OCMULGEE NATIONAL MONUMENT

A BRIEF HISTORY WITH FIELD NOTES

MERCER UNIVERSITY PRESS

Endowed by

TOM WATSON BROWN
and
THE WATSON-BROWN FOUNDATION, INC.

OCMULGEE NATIONAL MONUMENT

A BRIEF HISTORY WITH FIELD NOTES

MATTHEW JENNINGS

GORDON JOHNSTON

MERCER UNIVERSITY PRESS 2018

MUP/ P557

© 2018 by Mercer University Press
Published by Mercer University Press
1501 Mercer University Drive
Macon, Georgia 31207
All rights reserved

9 8 7 6 5 4 3 2 1

Books published by Mercer University Press are printed on acid-free paper that meets the requirements of the American National Standard for Information Sciences—Permanence of Paper for Printed Library Materials.

ISBN 978-0-88146-647-8

Cataloging-in-Publication Data is available from the Library of Congress

Book design by Burt&Burt
Text set using Consantia and Frutiger type.

MISSISSIPPIAN HOUSE Mississippianism, a broad set of cultural traits, including the construction of large earthen mounds, originated in the Mississippi River Valley and radiated outward in the years following 1,000 CE. The rectangular outline left behind by rotting postholes indicates the presence of a Mississippian house at Ocmulgee. (Courtesy National Park Service, Ocmulgee National Monument.)

FOR EVERYONE
WHO HAS HELD OCMULGEE DEAR,
BUT ESPECIALLY MUSKOGEE PEOPLE
EVERYWHERE,

AND FOR LONNIE DAVIS—
OCMULGEE COULD NOT HOPE
FOR A TRUER FRIEND.

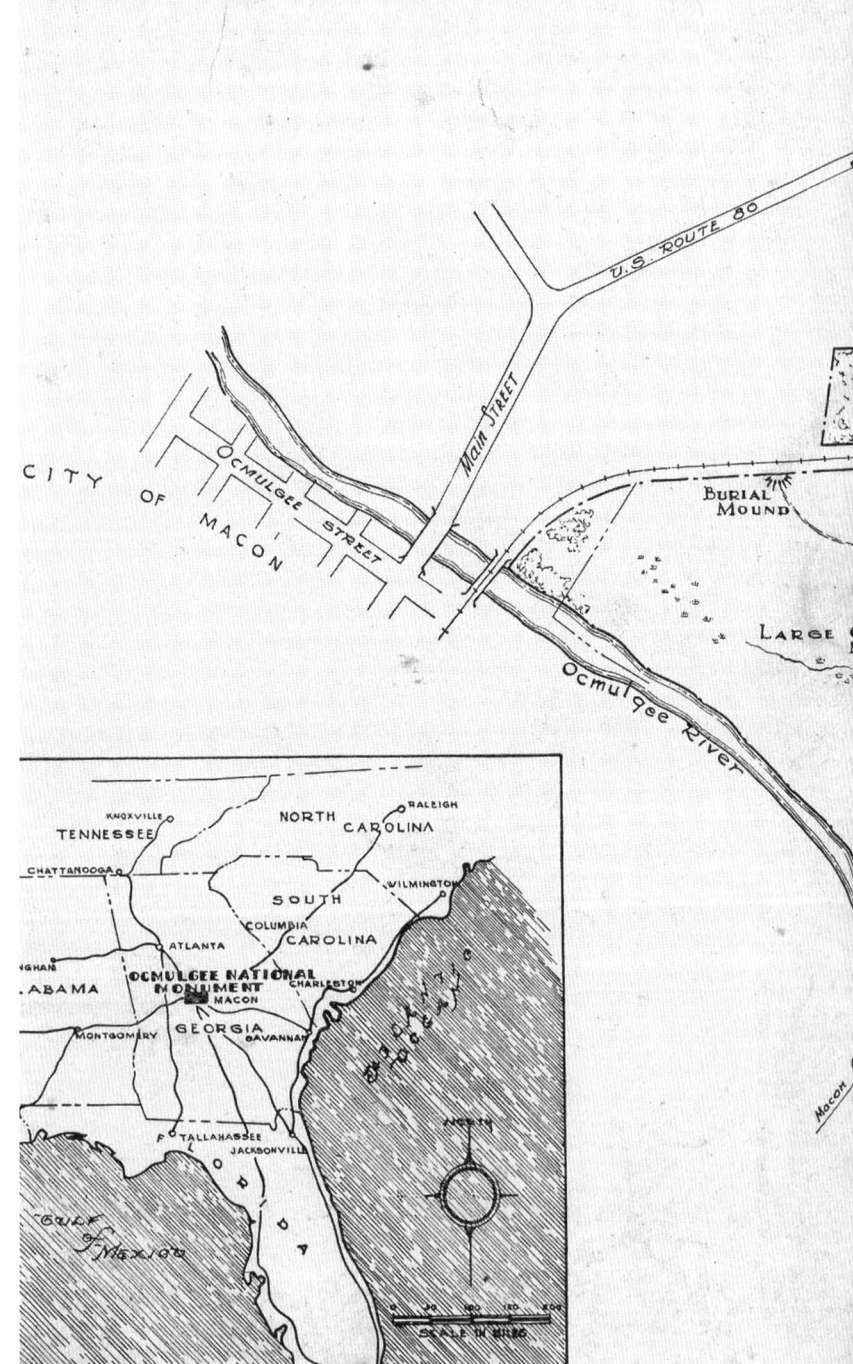

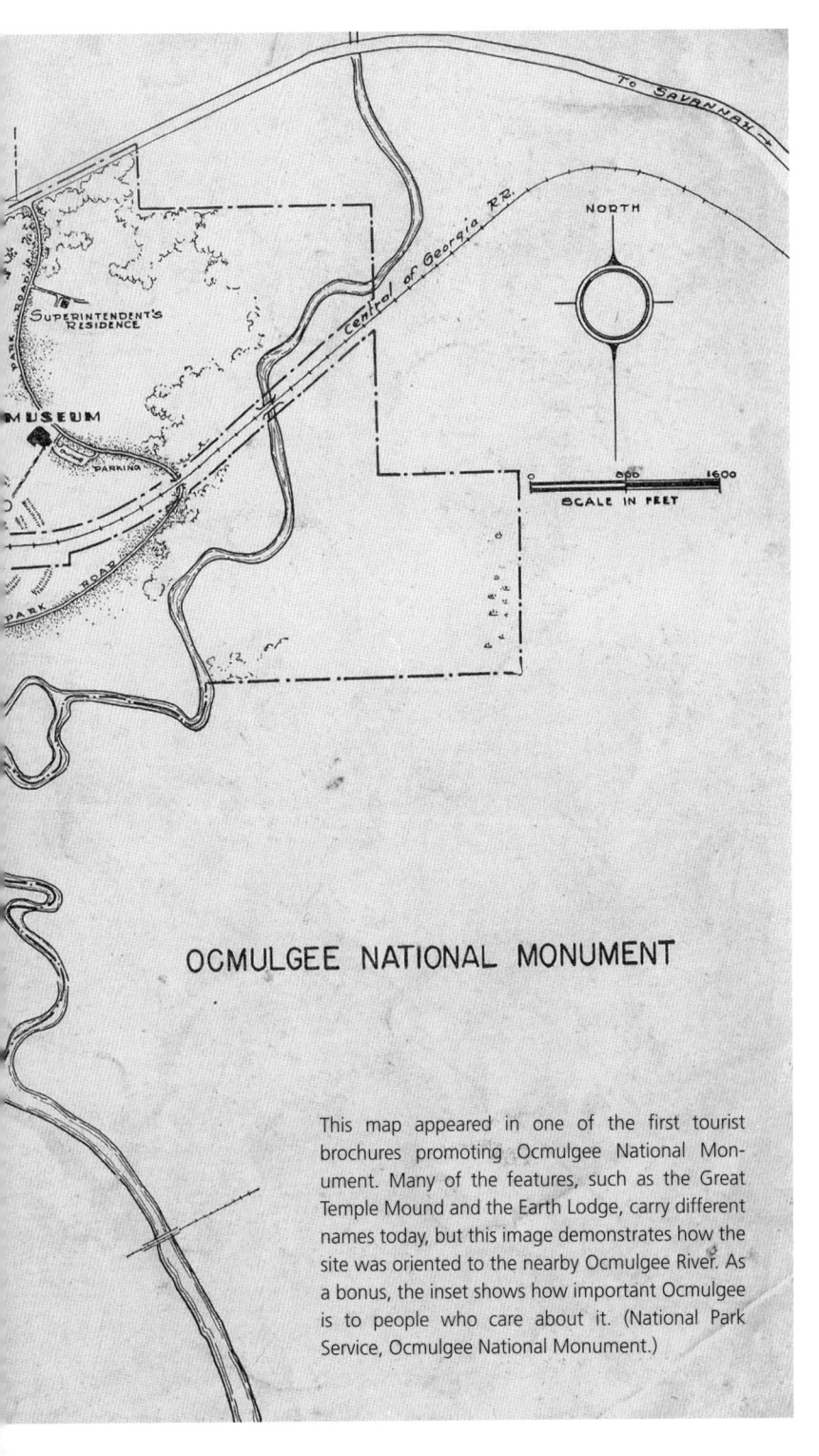

OCMULGEE NATIONAL MONUMENT

This map appeared in one of the first tourist brochures promoting Ocmulgee National Monument. Many of the features, such as the Great Temple Mound and the Earth Lodge, carry different names today, but this image demonstrates how the site was oriented to the nearby Ocmulgee River. As a bonus, the inset shows how important Ocmulgee is to people who care about it. (National Park Service, Ocmulgee National Monument.)

CONTENTS

ABOUT THE BOOK'S ORIGIN, STYLE, AND FOCUS / xiii

A NOTE ON TERMINOLOGY / xv

ACKNOWLEDGMENTS / xvii

PART 1: INTRODUCTION AND OVERVIEW / 1

PART 2: ARRIVING AND FORGING SOCIETIES / 13

PART 3: MAKING MONUMENTS / 31

PART 4: SITTING DOWN / 63

PART 5: LOSING AND FINDING OCMULGEE / 99

PART 6: KEEPING OCMULGEE / 135

PART 7: OCMULGEE TO OKMULGEE / 169

SOURCES AND FURTHER READING / 179

INDEX / 191

ABOUT THE BOOK'S ORIGIN, STYLE, AND FOCUS

Like the Ocmulgee River that first drew human beings here at least 12,000 years ago, this book bubbled up from a confluence. While the Ocmulgee forms at the meeting of the South, Yellow, and Alcovy Rivers (now under the waters of Lake Jackson), this slim historical guide to Ocmulgee National Monument in Macon, Georgia, and to the river nearby came together as a result of my meeting and coming to know my co-author Matt Jennings in Ocmulgee National Monument Association board meetings in 2013. At the time, I had been visiting the mounds three to five times a week for about a year as the monument's writer in residence. I had also been reading extensively about the mounds. Matt suggested books and gave me an extra copy of G. D. Pope's out-of-print guide to the park, which led to a conversation about the need for an updated version of such a guide. As a historian who had already written, published, and presented conference papers about the monument, and who had visited the Muscogee nation in Oklahoma, Matt was eminently qualified to update the history and archaeology in a new guide. For my part, I wanted to engage the park more subjectively, through my own experience of its earthworks, woods, river, artifacts, and wildlife, through native stories, and through imagining the experiences of others. Matt's style and approach are quite distinct from my own. My portions of the guide—called "field notes" because most of them I scribbled in my notebook in the park—are impressionistic, sensory, and momentary. Matt's pages are precise, concrete, and historical. We hope that the creative tension between our approaches keeps the book interesting and gives the reader depth of field about Ocmulgee—a balanced awareness (a confluence, even) of what this place has meant to human beings for many centuries and of what it continues to mean as its natural and anthropological life goes on.

Throughout the book, Matt and I have used the word Ocmulgee to refer to Ocmulgee National Monument, including the less-visited Lamar site across Interstate 16 from the park. When we refer to "the" Ocmulgee, we are talking about the river of that name which extends well above and below Macon, where the park is located.

—Gordon Johnston

A NOTE ON TERMINOLOGY

The words *Muscogee, Muskogee,* and *Muskogean* all appear in the text which follows, and the similarity between them may cause confusion. Muskogean refers to a large language family of the American Southeast, and occasionally to the people who spoke it in ancient times. Muskogean languages include Muskogee, Alabama, Koasati (or Coasati), Hitchiti (Mikasuki), Apalachee, Choctaw, and Chickasaw. The Muskogee language became the lingua franca of trade and diplomacy among a diverse coalition of peoples in present-day Georgia and Alabama in the years surrounding European colonization, and many of the people living on the Ocmulgee River in the late seventeenth century were native speakers or had become fluent. Whether or not these people who shared a language and a river drainage considered themselves a nation at this time has been a matter of scholarly debate. The English lumped them all together as "Creek Indians" because of their settlements on Ochese (which itself appears in various records as the Ocheese or Uchisi, and is now known as the Ocmulgee River). Today, the name of the Muscogee (Creek) Nation pays homage to both the language that bound the people together and the body of water near which they lived when they discovered the English. *Muscogee* and *Muskogee* are alternate spellings of the same word, a self-applied term to identify Muskogee people (*ma·skó·ki* or the shortened *maskó·ki* are rendered *Maskoke* and *Mvskoke*, respectively, in the traditional Creek spelling system). One does not have to read very deeply into oral traditions, history, or anthropology to recognize the myriad of alternate spellings of many of these terms. We recognize this complex situation, but we tried to make things clear at the same time. In the history which follows, we employ *Muskogee* to reference the language and the people, and *Muscogee* to refer to the modern Creek polity.

ACKNOWLEDGMENTS

Ocmulgee National Monument: A Brief History with Field Notes is not a very long book, but it was long in the making. I'm grateful to Marc Jolley at Mercer University Press for his patience, and I hope the result is worth the wait. The National Park Service, the current stewards of Ocmulgee, have been unfailingly helpful in providing access to the site's archives, and they have provided me opportunities to speak. Everyone at Ocmulgee has been hospitable and generous with their time, but Superintendent Jim David, Jim Branan, Sarah Reynolds, and Angela Bates were especially so. Lonnie Davis, cultural resources specialist, stands out, even among this stellar crew. From my sheepish early visits to Ocmulgee to more recent trips as a frantic mid-career professor, Lonnie has shared his deep knowledge of and passion for the site.

A handful of too-short visits to the Muscogee (Creek) Nation in Okmulgee, Oklahoma, and correspondence with Creek citizens and officials have convinced me that there is more work to be done to deepen the connection between the Creeks and their ancestral homeland. Perhaps this book might play some small role in that ongoing process. Thanks (*mvto*) to Principle Chief James Floyd, Odette Freeman, Johnnie Jacobs, Justin Giles, Christina Good Voice, RaeLynn

Butler, and the late Alfred Berryhill for all they've taught me. For the archaeological sections, I drew heavily on papers and comments from the Southeastern Archaeological Conference (SEAC) 2014 meeting as well as a few other sources. The works are listed in the "sources and further reading" section, but I would like to extend special thanks to Sarah Love, Jerald Ledbetter, and Benjamin Steere, and particulary Stephen Hammock and Daniel Bigman for sharing their expertise.

Thanks to my students and colleagues at Middle Georgia State University for both causing and putting up with digression after digression about Ocmulgee's history. Thanks also to the Ocmulgee Archaeological Society, SEAC, the Historic Macon Foundation, the Georgia Association of Historians, and the Native American and Indigenous Studies Association, all of which provided chances to speak about Ocmulgee. The Ocmulgee National Monument Association, especially Terry Jones, Lisa Lemon, and Billie Coleman have been so supportive as well, from covering the cost of images to introducing me to Gordon Johnston. Though he's too humble to say as much, Gordon is a gifted writer who taught me to see Ocmulgee from a variety of angles. Finally, none of this would be possible without the support of my friends and family. Susan and our sons, Henry and Oliver, have borne the brunt of my ceaseless Ocmulgee-related chatter over the past couple of years, and I thank them for allowing me to run things by them first.

—Matthew Jennings

Both my relationship with Ocmulgee National Monument and the writing I have done about it have grown from a web of relationships for which I am abidingly grateful. First thanks must go to my partner in the word, Matt Jennings, whose amiability, relationships, organizational skills, and deep historical knowledge are the foundation of this guide. His command of the history and archaeology of the monument freed me to report on its bluebirds, weather, spirits, and stories.

I echo Matt's gratitude to Jim David (who was enthusiastic about my serving as writer in residence at the monument), Lonnie Davis (a human archive of cultural and archaeological knowledge), Jim Branan, and Angela Bates. I add to the list Guy LaChine, who first suggested I write about my own experience of Ocmulgee National Monument's landscape rather than strictly about its past. I also echo Matt's appreciation of the friendship and hard work of my fellow ONM Association Board members—especially Lisa Lemon (who first involved me with the board and whose excellent recruitment for the annual Ocmulgee Indian Celebration acquainted me with Muscogee and other First Nations dancers, singers, storytellers, shell carvers, artists, and souls), Terry Jones (our fearless and often funny leader), and the ever humane and receptive Dr. Lindsay Holliday (whose dental office is a secret salon of Fall Line art and culture).

I am grateful to William Harjo for letting me, my students, and my children share in the Muscogee cultural inheritance that he continues to pass along and to the Touch the Earth Dancers and the many other indigenous dancers, drummers, and singers through whom native culture thrives and sustains its ancient Ocmulgee roots. Thanks to Marc Jolley for his belief in this guide and his patience as it slowly came together and to the College of Liberal Arts at Mercer University, which afforded a sabbatical that let me canoe the Ocmulgee, Oconee, and Altamaha; read about the human communities this watershed has prospered; and begin to draft my portion of this guide. Thanks to Don Ream for paddling most of those rivers with me.

My partner, Pam Johnston, held down the home front when I was on the rivers and was my best critic. My daughter, Emma, and my sons, Micah and Graham, have kept me company at every Ocmulgee Indian Festival (and on many hikes in the park) since 2003. Their curiosity, support, and receptiveness to my ramblings have been an enormous help. In a similar vein, thanks go to my students at Mercer for their intelligent engagement, thought-provoking questions, and effective field work collecting and transcribing oral stories.

I would be remiss not to acknowledge the excellent work of the writers and scholars whose names and works are listed in the "For Further Reading" portion of this guide. They laid the trail that Matt and I have tried to maintain and extend, and for that we are thankful.

—Gordon Johnston

Many of the photographs included in the book are part of the collection owned by Ocmulgee National Monument and the National Park Service, and several photographs are of objects on display at Ocmulgee. The authors appreciate the National Park Service's generosity in allowing them to publish the pictures, and are especially grateful to Lonnie Davis, who manages the curatorial department at Ocmulgee.

Gordon and Matt both wish to thank Leslie Andres, whose keen copyediting saved us some embarrassment, and Sharman Ayoub, whose photograph graces the cover.

OCMULGEE NATIONAL MONUMENT

PART 1

INTRODUCTION AND OVERVIEW

This place, this "Ocmulgee," has captured people's imaginations for a long time. Chances are, if you're reading these words, the site has touched you in some way, too. We do not know what the earliest inhabitants of the site called it, but we do know that they benefited from the nearby river and the rich and varied landscape along its banks. We do not know what the people who built the mounds that command the surrounding landscape called it either, for that matter. Eventually, the river, as well as a handful of towns in Georgia, Alabama, and Oklahoma would bear the name. It was probably bestowed by speakers of the Hitchiti variant of the larger Muskogean language family, and has been translated to mean "bubbling waters," "boiling waters," and "bubbling up of water from a spring," in various eras. Whatever the word "Ocmulgee" has meant over the centuries, the place has meant quite a lot to the people who have called it home.

As soon as human beings found their way into what is now Middle Georgia, they recognized the beauty and utility of the Ocmulgee River near the fall line, at which point faster flowing water from the uplands descends and winds more slowly toward the ocean. The human fascination continues to the present as thousands upon thousands of students, tourists, hikers, bird watchers, and other nature lovers visit the site each year. At almost every discernable point of the human past, from 12,000 years ago until today, somebody has seen Ocmulgee as a worthy place to live, trade, farm, or fight for. To be sure, some of these occupations were more dramatic and more widely recognized than others: Mississippian-era (moundbuilders of the era from about 800–1600 CE) people constructed earthworks that have stood for a thousand years. Some of these occupations were outright destructive: as Macon grew into a center of commerce in the nineteenth century, two railroad lines sliced through the site, the first constructed largely by enslaved labor from nearby plantations; in addition, several plantations, worked by enslaved women and men, also made their mark on the landscape and the people of Ocmulgee in the years before the Civil War. Some of the occupations are more dimly understood than others even though they're more recent than either the mounds or the railroads: in the 1950s, again in the 1970s, and off and on since the 1990s, Muscogee (Creek) citizens and other Native people have reclaimed Ocmulgee as sacred ground and reasserted their deep connection to the place.

OCMULGEE FIELD NOTE

BOY IN THE RIVER

The boy lies down in the river, his body fitting perfectly into its clear gold shallows. His shoulder blades graze the grainy bottom as the water's surface laves his chin, cool as a bedsheet. He is tucked in but not still. The river, diminished by the drought, is a concentrated current. He is at rest, but has to push his fingers into the sand or be carried away. He floats in a delicious betweenness, face-up to the sky, rippling like a flag, knowing he could let go, savoring his grip and his immersion in a motion that grows and shrinks, clouds and clears, and never stops. The river has always been here and leaving. It will be when he is gone. There will be the same minnows flickering like a volley of arrows through the inch-deep edge. There will be the same shelving rocks like unearthed stacks of fossilized books, the same one-strand swing, though the rope and the sycamore branch it is knotted to will be different. Through these small renewals the place remains itself. (The boy could not say this. His knowing it is not the same as his thinking it.) The pleasure he feels in being baptized in all this is not the pleasure of stasis, but of constancy and circulation. What is here now will be again—right now is an again. *He has heard he can't swim in the same river twice. He takes this as a comment on his nature, not the river's. The river will repeat itself. The boy just won't be here to hear it, which is why he enjoys listening now.*

The river today lets him be on the surface and at the bottom and halfway between the two all at the same time. He wants to remember this so he can tell his friends, but he probably won't. Retention is not the way of a river, which constantly tears at its margins and pushes at anything that tries to keep its place, and when you're in a river you tend to do as the river does. You flow. Thoughts stream, as do sensations and memories. The present constantly overwrites the just-past. There is no stillness to pin anything to. When you fish, you have to keep re-casting in order to keep your cork in the same place. The boy does not worry that he will forget. On the river, every moment promises more of what has happened before. Any jot missed or forgotten will be there minutely altered to be witnessed again. Nothing is lost. People are not the keepers.

Because he is not the keeper, the boy can be a basker. He can roll onto his stomach and see the river's skin wobble at eye-level, like an alligator would. He can feel the water undulate along his arms and legs, can dig his toes into the mica grit of the bottom and detect along his insoles the dissipating cloud of silt he has churned up. He can steel himself not to twitch when the bream nip his freckles. Because he is not a keeper, he is kept. Like a sabbath. Like a small thing found, tucked into a warm pocket, and carried away.

* * * * *

Native communities, both ancestral and contemporary, and amateur and professional historians and archaeologists have told their own versions of Ocmulgee's history before. The chronicles of the Hernando de Soto expedition, which tore through the Southeast from 1539 to 1543, mention the mounds and the people briefly, but, fortunately for their Native hosts, the Spanish moved on quickly in search of riches. The earliest recorded use of Ocmulgee as a site for understanding history came from the pen of an anonymous soldier who rode with James Oglethorpe in 1739. He wrote of "three Mounts raised by the Indians over three of their Great Kings who were killed in the Wars." Since there's no mention of which Indians, which kings, or which wars, the account is of limited use. William Bartram, the Philadelphia-born naturalist and traveler, visited Ocmulgee in the 1770s. After describing the site, Bartram noted that "If we give credit to the account the Creeks give of themselves, this place is remarkable for being the first town or settlement where they sat down (as they term it) or established themselves after their emigration from the west." This Creek story, filtered through Bartram, is crucial to understanding Ocmulgee's role in Muskogee history and is an early indication of just how important the site was to Native people.

Muskogee-speakers would continue to allude to Ocmulgee's centrality in their history even after they were pressured to give up their claim to the land. Nineteenth-century white accounts of Ocmulgee's history veer crazily in quality, from a *Macon Telegraph* editor's suggesting that an ancient ocean had erected the largest mound to the reasonably accurate renderings of the amateur archaeologist Charles Colcock Jones Jr. in his 1873 *Antiquities of the Southern Indians, Particularly of the Georgia Tribes*. As the scholarly establishment began to digest the huge number of important finds emanating from the New Deal-era excavations, scattered professional-quality works began to appear, the most important being Charles Fairbanks's *Archeology of the Funeral Mound*, initially published in 1956 and reissued in 1980 and 2003, and Carol Mason's 1963 dissertation, *The Archaeology of Ocmulgee Old Fields, Macon, Georgia*, which the University of Alabama Press published in 2005. *Archeology of the Funeral Mound* and *The Archaeology of Ocmulgee Old Fields* are exceptionally valuable contributions to our understanding of Ocmulgee. Indeed, both are still on sale at the museum's gift shop as of this writing, and they are required reading for serious students of Ocmulgee's history. But both can be extremely technically specific at times, and each focuses most of its energy on a single aspect of the site: Mound C, or the Funeral Mound, in Fairbanks's case, and the Trading Post in Mason's. It wasn't until 1994 that the results of a 1986 Ocmulgee archaeology conference at Mercer University finally emerged. The resulting volume, *Ocmulgee Archaeology, 1936–1986*, was an instant classic. It brought veterans of the 1930s digs and recent experts in Southeastern archaeology and history together to produce a work of lasting quality (and another ironclad requirement on the all-Ocmulgee syllabus). But, at $50 in hardcover, it remained inaccessible to a larger audience, and in any event, some members of that larger audience might have shied away from the more jargon-laden chapters. What about works aimed at the general public, well read and typically curious, but lacking the technical training to decipher writing by experts for experts? The answer will take us back to the years following World War II, right around the time the Museum and Visitor Center opened to the public.

G. D. Pope Jr., also known as "Gus," served as chief archaeologist at Ocmulgee in the 1950s and had a lot on his plate. His daily duties entailed shepherding dignitaries and tourists around the grounds of the monument as well as curating and maintaining museum exhibits. He also coordinated or supervised occasional archaeological work on the park's sprawling acreage. His official post must have involved a massive amount of paperwork, given the records left behind in filing cabinets in the curatorial department at Ocmulgee, as well as in other repositories, primarily the National Archives branch in Philadelphia, which houses many National Park Service documents. But around the edges of his various reports, one can catch glimpses of something else: Pope believed that the public deserved a lengthier, more modern introduction to the treasures of Ocmulgee than the previous National Park Service publications, little more than brochures, really, though he struggled mightily to find the time to work on it. As early as February 1952, Pope reported that he "expect[ed] to devote all available time during the coming month to work on preparation of the new Handbook." Later reports proved this to be difficult: "it is hoped that more tangible progress will be made," "the handbook will receive as much time as can be spared," "I think there will be time...to resume work on the handbook," and so on. Pope persevered, and the results were beautiful.

In 1956, *Ocmulgee*, National Park Service Historical Handbook No. 24, took its place alongside brief histories of much better-known park sites, which to that point included such stars as Gettysburg, the Statue of Liberty, Independence National Historical Park, and Jamestown. Pope's *Ocmulgee* perfectly distilled the work archaeologists had

The cover of G.D. Pope's 1956 *Ocmulgee Handbook*.
(National Park Service, Ocmulgee National Monument.)

carried out at the site in prior decades and conveyed that specialized knowledge to a broad public in plain language, from "The American Indian" and "Man Comes to Georgia" to "Ocmulgee Old Fields." Though the terminology has changed, the chronology follows a track that will be familiar to modern readers and visitors to the museum. "Wandering Hunters" have become Paleoindians, "Shellfish Eaters" denoted the region's Archaic-era peoples, and "Master Farmers" are now Mississippians. Apart from the fact that the book's timeline essentially ends in 1828, with a brief foray into the creation of the national monument in the 1930s, *Ocmulgee* shows its age in other ways. Not only have new archaeological finds and frameworks altered and improved our understanding of the site, the practice of history has changed in the intervening decades as well. Citizens of contemporary Native nations, including the Muscogee (Creek) Nation of eastern Oklahoma, have changed the way historians, Native and non-Native alike, understand the Native American past. The changes in historical practice have manifested themselves in many ways, including the increasing attention paid to the legacy of removal and colonialism, particularly as it relates to struggles over land, sacred space, and identity. In recent years, historians have expressed a great deal more interest in matters of gender and the lives of ordinary people. All of these shifts have enriched our understanding of the past and have influenced this book profoundly. It is not fair to mock archaeologists and historians of the 1950s for writing like archaeologists and historians wrote in the 1950s, but it is fair to point out the limitations in these earlier works, just as we believe someone will point out the limitations in our work in the future. Pope's handbook was reprinted in 1961, and that edition stands as the last published attempt to encapsulate all the eras of the park's history in a book-length treatment intended for a wide readership. Since 1961, several publications have covered some aspect of Ocmulgee's history. Some truly remarkable works have dealt with aspects of Ocmulgee's archaeological importance, and a handful of National Park Service-produced volumes have illuminated the park's administrative history and cultural significance of some of its key features, such as the Earth Lodge and the Visitor Center, but no publication since Pope's has assayed to bridge the gap between the scholarly and popular and cover recent developments at the site.

As this brief historiographical sketch shows, we are not, by a long shot, the first people to try to chronicle Ocmulgee's lengthy history. We have relied on oral traditions, travelers' accounts, and historical and archaeological research stretching from the very dawn of those disciplines to the most recent scholarship available. We also hope that our book goes beyond these previous efforts in some key ways. We have tried to do right by the site in the pages that follow, but we also recognize that we will not be the last people to write on this rich subject. We intend this slim volume not just as a guide to Ocmulgee's past but also as a resource for future scholars, who can mine the "for further reading" section at the book's end to prompt questions we could never ask, and perhaps propel a new generation of scholarship that will eclipse this meager offering.

Muskogee-speakers have been one of the most significant influences on Ocmulgee from the seventeenth century to the present, and the book's seven-part organization reflects that. The importance of the number seven manifests itself in many ways in Creek cosmology, from one grouping of the celestial bodies known to ancestral Creeks (the sun, moon, and five planets) to the seven visible stars of the *Kolas-Coklofkv*, or Pleiades, to the seven directions (the four cardinal directions, as well as others pointing upward, downward, and inward). It seemed fitting to divide this concise history into seven parts, even if they ranged widely in terms of their periodization. Following the first part, the introduction and overview, the second part, "Arriving and Forging Societies," treats the arrival of human beings and describes the communities they created during what archaeologists call the Paleoindian, Archaic, and Woodland eras (12,000 or more years ago to about 1,000 years ago). Part 3, "Making Monuments," focuses on the Mississippian emergence at Ocmulgee, which unfolded in at least two phases between 1000 and 1600 CE, and featured some of the most spectacular architectural developments at the site. Part 4, "Sitting Down," begins with the dispersal of the Mississippian order, sped along by the invasion from Europe, and moves through the establishment of Muskogee towns and their response to the increasing presence of European powers, particularly the English, in their neighborhood. "Losing and

Finding Ocmulgee," the fifth part, sweeps through the era of the American War for Independence, the subsequent forced abandonment of Ocmulgee by Creeks in the early nineteenth century, and American "stewardship" (really exploitation) of the site in the following decades. It closes with the rediscovery of Ocmulgee's historical value by Maconites in the twentieth century, the founding of Ocmulgee National Monument, and the long-delayed opening of the Museum and Visitor Center. "Keeping Ocmulgee," part 6, goes significantly beyond previous histories by bringing the story of Ocmulgee into the more recent past. It follows the efforts of the Muscogee (Creek) Nation, the National Park Service, and the citizens of Macon since the 1950s. Though each of these entities had its own reasons for protecting and preserving Ocmulgee, they converged at key points, and Ocmulgee today bears the imprint of each of their various influences and stands as a testament to their labors. Finally, a brief epilogue, the seventh direction, as it were, will center readers within Ocmulgee and tie together the site's past, present, and future.

OCMULGEE FIELD NOTE

RUNNING ON OLD EARTH

Running Ocmulgee National Monument—better known since my grade school days as the Indian mounds—seemed irreverent to me until I read about the respect that the First Nations people living at the Lamar site had for fleet, enduring feet. The Spanish with Hernando de Soto reported native men who could run down deer—and learned the hard way how quickly these runners could pass news between towns and even chiefdoms. Later, the Muscogee fielded their swiftest men here to play their intensely competitive stick ball game—"the little brother of war"—town against town, with enormous wagers and sometimes a town's political autonomy riding on the result. Hearing these stories, I thought Ocmulgee might crave the drumming of human feet on its old earth. I thought the trails would take it in stride. On my first run in the park, little things seemed to validate the idea—the Clinton Street gate that was open that early morning seemed like a welcome, as did the keening of the red-tailed hawks that turned over the field just inside the boundary. I would not have heard the hawks had my iPod's battery not died as I entered the monument. The failure felt fortunate, like the agency of the place, or like an assertion that the mounds expected more than glancing attention. The park would accept my sweaty hustle down its spiral aisles through forest and along the bases of the mounds, but it had terms.

I had to be aware in the place—mindful of it. The monument couldn't be run like a loop of city sidewalk. Roots, briars, and uneven ground would trip, snag, and bruise the oblivious. The unexpected yellow jacket, snake, or mud hole would waylay him. Tear face-first through an orb weaver's web and you will feel spider legs tickling your ears, eyebrows, and nape all morning after. More important still was a mindfulness of the generations of human life that the place had nourished and the way those generations succeeded one another here, learning what this watershed would allow and what it would prosper, and developing a culture that honored these natural gifts and limits. I resolved to remember that a sequence of nations had taken root and grown here, learning how to live, die, marry, sing, play, farm, wage war, dance, pray, remember, heal, and cooperate communally. I resolved to read about them and to run with respect—to give myself up to the place and its memory and see what it taught me.

The attention I paid the woods and fields they reciprocated immediately. My lookout for sticks in the path yielded a dung beetle rolling her tidy brown ball, several red-eyed, black-bodied cicadas clapping their wings, and a king snake, all in the first few months. An eye leery of snakes makes out a terrapin under blackberry canes—or, better yet, ripe blackberries. These you stop for. Other sightings don't slow you a step. The wildflowers in the field across the railroad cut from the Great Temple Mound draw you down the path a step faster, like a crowd of spectators. The spider lilies in early spring are fewer and fiercer: among them you run from blossom to blossom, as if they hand you along. Autumns, I found myself running tree to particular tree across the park, their leaves like signal fires blazing one shade paler each day. Winter loops are sparer—trees twiggy and bare, white glitter in the stunned grass and on the streams, stiff as glass.

On winter runs at Ocmulgee, what you mostly see is yourself breathe. You carry this out with you. In diving into the depths of the history here, you see humanity breathe. This breath, personal and human, is the news you came for.

PART 2

ARRIVING AND FORGING SOCIETIES

Antonio C. Waring Jr., also known as "Tono," who would go on to become one of the leading archaeologists of the Southeast in spite of his medical training, was an unlucky undergraduate in the summer of 1935. Arthur Kelly, the young man's mentor, was supervising excavations near the Council Chamber (today's Earth Lodge) when an unnamed laborer uncovered one of the most important finds ever to be unearthed at Ocmulgee: a large portion of a fluted stone point, which archaeologists had recently come to call a Clovis point, after the town in New Mexico where the first one was found in 1932. Waring "just missed" this amazing event, and "spent the rest of the summer sitting on the edge of the excavations in the forlorn hope that more fluted points would be found." Though various cutting and scraping tools would also come to light that summer, no other Clovis points were forthcoming. Still, people recognized the significance of the

MACON PLATEAU CLOVIS POINT To date, this Clovis point remains the oldest artifact associated with Ocmulgee. Paleoindians prized sources of high-quality stone, and used points like this one to hunt big game. (Photo by Gordon Johnston from the collection of Ocmulgee National Monument.)

find immediately because it proved the antiquity of human occupation on the Macon Plateau. In a way, many of us who love Ocmulgee can relate to the frustration of young Tono. In spite of recent archaeological work, the earliest periods of Ocmulgee's history remain comparatively dimly understood, and we sit forlornly on the edge of a full understanding of this time, awaiting new discoveries.

PALEOINDIANS AT OCMULGEE

Archaeologists divide eastern North America's distant past into three broad periods: the Paleoindian (12,500 or more years ago to 10,000 years ago), the Archaic (10,000 years ago to 3,000 years ago), and the Woodland (3,000 years ago to 1,100 years ago). Specialists slice this chronology even more finely, with each period featuring an early, middle, and late division. People made their mark at Ocmulgee during each of these spans of time, and Ocmulgee, though to a lesser extent than some other Georgia sites, has added to our knowledge of life in the Southeast during each of them. The people whom archaeologists named Paleoindians arrived in Georgia not too long after they arrived in North America. Scholars dispute precisely how many thousands of years ago people came to North America, but in recent years something approaching a consensus has emerged. The Americas were peopled in multiple waves by diverse groups of people moving overland and along the Pacific coast. The earliest groups may have arrived as many as 20,000 years ago (this is on the high end, and not without controversy), and the most recent arrived between 8,000 and 4,000 years ago. The presence of Paleoindians in the Southeast is clear—though the date of their arrival is anything but. The archaeologists of the Topper Site, a quarry on the South Carolina side of the Savannah River, claim an antiquity of 50,000 years, but the archaeological community has been hesitant to embrace this early date. In spring 2016, Florida State University archaeologists published findings from the Aucilla River near the Gulf of Mexico. At the Page-Ladson site, divers found stone tools among mastodon remains, and subsequently placed the date of the assemblage at 14,500 years before the present. As far as we can tell, the Paleo-era occupation at Ocmulgee, while extremely old, is not *that* old.

The initial excavations directed by Kelly in the 1930s were huge and ranged downward through a large swath of the site's human history. Still, they uncovered only the single aforementioned Clovis point and an associated cache of cutting tools and scrapers dating to the Paleoindian and Archaic periods. Subsequent archaeological work at Ocmulgee, particularly in excavations connected with the construction of Interstate 16 in the early 1960s (more on this later), led to the discovery of two Dalton points, known to have been used in the Late Paleoindian period. Such limited evidence promted the conclusion that these first people were probably just passing through. However, in the intervening decades, our knowledge of the Paleoindian world *outside* of Ocmulgee has increased, thanks to excavations and interactions between avocational archaeologists and professionals to build databases of sites (the Society for Georgia Archaeology's Paleoindian Artifact Recording Project and Paleoindian Projectile Point survey have led the way in this regard), and it may be time to revisit our earlier assumptions.

An early 1980s count of Paleoindian points noted only ten examples from the entire state of Georgia (neighboring Alabama and Florida boasted well over 1,000 each in the same survey). Subsequent surveys have raised the

DALTON POINT Dalton points, which date to the late Paleoindian period, are lance-shaped (or lanceolate) and concave at the base. (Photo by Susan Jennings from the collection of Ocmulgee National Monument.)

number significantly. As of this writing, there are more than 400 documented Paleoindian points and almost 1900 Early Archaic examples, identified at a range of site types including short-term camps, quarry camps, residential camps, and kill sites. Ocmulgee appears to fall into the short-term camp designation, but our understanding of this earliest period remains imperfect.

For much of the twentieth century, anthropologists and historians, blinded by Eurocentric biases at the core of their disciplines, disparaged the considerable achievements of the first people in North America. Scholarly and popular interpretations of Paleoindians stressed their supposedly primitive and strange ways. Pope, in his 1956 guidebook, praised their "considerable ingenuity" and "hard work," but he also resorted to describing the people by the things they lacked, such as pottery and bows and arrows. He betrayed deep-seated biases when he noted their "simple stage of culture" and compared them to "all primitive peoples today." In the past few years, a fuller, more complicated picture of early life in the Southeast has begun to emerge, and Ocmulgee has played an important, if not a leading, role in that emergence. For much of the past century, it was taken for granted that small bands of Paleoindians ranged over vast territories, following big game, which formed the basis of their diet and informed many aspects of their societies. Such groups would have been essentially nomadic, geared to follow the wandering whims of megafauna, like mastodons. New models have attempted to explain the distribution of various sorts of artifacts, and now it seems much more likely that once a group moved into a resource-rich area, a core of the group remained there, while smaller parties might explore surrounding areas to see what they offered. Rather than denigrating the abilities of these first people, it is more appropriate to praise their skill as hunters and their ability to create diverse subsistence economies that took advantage of a wide array of resources. North America in their time was cooler and wetter (though warming rapidly) than it is today, and a fluctuating coastline and other environmental changes required constant vigilance and savvy to survive. We know that there were core areas of human occupation on Florida's Gulf Coast extending into South Georgia and from the Savannah River to the Atlantic. It seems safe to assume that Ocmulgee, with access to both watersheds and a rich fall-line environment, could have served as a way station of sorts, one capable of supporting semi-permanent settlements. Indeed, though no large-scale kill sites have come to light near Ocmulgee, evidence of other types of occupations continues to accumulate from the Wallace Reservoir site on the Oconee River, the Russell Reservoir site on the Savannah River, and the Feronia Locality, an assemblage of flaked stone artifacts near the Big Bend of the Ocmulgee, in Coffee County.

ARCHAIC-ERA OCMULGEE

We do not know the names by which Paleoindians identified themselves and their communities. "Paleoindian" seems as good a term as any though it may mask a considerable amount of diversity. It is certainly superior to "Paleoamerican," which is used by those who wish to assert an ancient, and likely mythical, connection between Europe and the Americas. These early arrivals might not have divided their history into sharply defined epochs, as many archaeologists and historians have done. Our approach to Ocmulgee and its history, while divided chronologically for purposes of organizational clarity, aims for a more nuanced approach. At Ocmulgee, and in the Southeast generally, the lines between "prehistory" (rightfully falling out of favor) and history are blurred, and the lines between the Paleoindian and Archaic eras are similarly fuzzy.

Early interpretations of the Archaic Era stressed what its earliest people lacked, namely pottery and horticulture, and emphasized the shift in diet from big game to smaller game and marine food sources. Ocmulgee's park literature, signage in the 1950s-era Visitor Center, and Pope's handbook used the phrase "Shellfish Eaters" to describe the people who inhabited Ocmulgee between 10,000 and 3,000 years ago. As a whole, the Archaic period, as lengthy and significant as it was, suffers because it remains pinched between two supposedly more significant stories, the story of how human beings came to the Americas and the story of how recognizable Native societies formed. One scholar, writing against this grain, has gone so far as to describe the Archaic Era as a "long interval of nothingness."

OCMULGEE FIELD NOTE

NEEDS AND CHOICES

Their needs make their choices, these people who move in small groups through the green shadows of ancient forests and along the banks of the river. Since their needs are met by wild animals, they follow them into the places where human and animal prosperities meet and cannot be distinguished one from the other. The berries, roots, nuts, muscadines, greens, fish, and mussels that nourish the animals—deer, buffalo, bears, and birds—also nourish the people. The woods and river are communal, a table that feeds the whole community of creatures. The people eat the animals also, believing as they do so that they are taking in not only nourishment, but the animals' attri-

butes as well. The people respect and aspire to have the superior vision, agility, speed, and strength of the animals that let themselves be harvested by hunters.

The people live in the animals' skins, stitching hides into clothing and shelter, making of their bones flutes, needles, weapons, and glue. The men are jeweled with their feathers, claws, and teeth.

The people know and acknowledge all these gifts given by animals. As they receive, they return thanks, never mistaking animal generosity for human mastery. The animals know the value of their lives and they make the people work for these gifts. The people must learn the animals' ways—their migrations and match-makings, the raising of the young, their responses to threats and weather. Animals are to them a living scripture that must be read, respected, remembered. The people's lives depend on it. They tell stories of these animals and paint their images on themselves and on their walls to acknowledge the animals' powers—the panther's and owl's vision, the woodpecker's power to pierce trees, the deer's speed and leap. The people see in these abilities, offices, and disciplines fit models for themselves. They revere and identify with animals; over time, the people come to organize themselves socially into clans based on powerful animals whose attributes clan members must live up to. The clan brings the animal's qualities to the larger community and perpetuates them there.

The people's needs make their choices and since the animals meet the people's needs, the people discern and value the animals' needs. They note what trees whitetails strip bark from in winter, what blooms bring hummingbirds back each spring. They note the mouse and vole skulls that hatch from the horned owl's pellets. They divine the motive of the congregating alligators. They learn. They remember.

They feel for the strands of a complicated web in which every life hangs connected. The people are not at its center, but in its margins, where they are safer. From these margins the people watch and sense the animals as they act in the delicate balance. No animal is so small that its will, effort, and abilities don't matter.

The web stretches beyond the periphery of the people's vision. Their stories acknowledge that there are gaps and forgettings in the people's knowledge. They feel for the web's strands along these edges of their knowledge, seeing in their dreams where the cross-threads are anchored. They watch and discern. They experiment.

As they learn, they make use of the knowledge. Rather than simply gathering nuts, greens, and fruits, they come to discern the sort of places and conditions in which these foods prosper. They seek out such places and make nurseries of them. They settle around them. They take note of how different earths and different woods and canes behave in fire. They learn the uses of gourds and clay. They make containers for water, for seed, for acorns, for meat. These small containments lead to larger ones. They further map the land in the people's memory—mark the locations of clay lenses along rivers, salt licks. The web informs the map and the map informs the web. The people's needs still make their choices, but their choices become wiser. They begin to weave a web of the strands they most need—where these strands meet, they make a home.

* * * * *

Speaking broadly, Archaic-era populations were slightly more sedentary and denser than those of their supposedly nomadic ancestors. The climate was changing rapidly during their time, and communities began to differentiate themselves based on the adaptations they made to their particular environments, as the story goes. This synthesis carries us only so far because we now understand the Paleoindian period in a way that accounts for diverse origins and adaptations. We also must acknowledge the cultural dimensions, the human element, sorely lacking in earlier interpretations, which took a decidedly ecologically determinist angle. The environment in which people found themselves mattered, but so did the people and their ideas. Monumental architecture, sedentary village life, horticulture, and pottery were, in the past, taken to signal the onset of a new age, the Woodland Era, but all were present in the Southeast during the Archaic Era (witness the massive earthworks at Poverty Point in Louisiana, an Archaic era site), and at least one of these traits, pottery, appeared quite early at Ocmulgee.

OCMULGEE FIELD NOTE

A STONE OWL

April 18, 2017

The stone owl calls to my hand. It strikes me with its features first. It looks at me frankly, directly, with an awareness that feels more than animal, that has calm strength. Its small size makes the owl personal in scale—graspable, weighty, just the right size to fit my human hand. The varied textures of its fired clay surface—ruddy as a fresh-baked biscuit at its face and breast, ashy along its back and sides—invite touch. Like real animals, it seems profoundly self-possessed.

When I take it up, it doesn't feel as heavy as its stony coolness suggests it should be. Turning it over, I find that it's hollow—if it weren't, the clay would probably have exploded in the fire that transformed it. This explains the owl's lightness, but deepens the mystery of the substance it has. I'm not sure what it says, but it says it with authority.

It dawns on me that the first thing it says is owl. *This stone bird's hollowness—its light, deft packing of enormous power—echoes a real owl's. The elegant fold of its wings, its repose, the smoothness of its unruffled stone feathers—all are true to the living raptor, whose edges are softened to give it silence for the hunt. The owl's "ears" are true to the animal's profile, too. Whoever made this representation knew the subject. That knowledge gives the statue power.*

The eyes—the feature that first drew me—need explaining. Now that I've spent time holding him I see that within his owl-ness—especially within his distinctly owly head—the defining part of the bird, his penetrating, concentric pupils, is not at all owl-like. The eyes are round, but the brows over them are not soft or feathery. They are bone, like human brows. Like human brows, they meet and slope down to form not the beak I expect to see but a nose, complete with a hint of nostrils. As the human and animal meet in these features, the face becomes suddenly strange. In my hand is the prayer of another people—a supplication for what the owl has, for vision that pierces moonless night.

In my own people's cosmology, this meeting is impossible. The human and animal worlds are different worlds, the former superior always to the latter. In my people's view, we think, therefore we are. Animals do not think, therefore they are not. In my people's world, if the human and animal worlds cross, the result is a freak or a mon-

ster—a werewolf, a harpy, a man-eating siren. Between our world and that of the animals there is a wall.

For the artist who shaped and fired this bird just the size for a hunter's grasp, in place of this wall there was something like a membrane—placental and permeable. Across and through this membrane, gifts could travel from the animals to the people. Powers could be passed back and forth. That membrane was approached with respect and ritual purification. To hold this owl is to touch the membrane. The weight of this owl is the weight of reverence, if only I can learn how to read it.

There is hope that I can. The people who revered this bird and my own people have grown from the same very old root. Buried in me, forgotten but not beyond remembering, is the wish to understand. The owl's call to the potter passes through him to me through this stone in my hand.

* * * * *

The Early and Middle Archaic periods of Ocmulgee's history are, and must remain, dimly understood, at least for the time being. The cache of tools found in association with the Clovis point was a mish-mash of Paleoindian and Early Archaic implements, and apart from this 1930s discovery, few remnants of the Early and Middle Archaic period have been excavated at Ocmulgee. That situation changes dramatically when it comes to the Late Archaic era (5,000 to 3,000 years ago). Work at several sites in and around Ocmulgee, including the Southeastern Plateau, a bluff near Mound C or the Funeral Mound, and the low-lying area south of the Great Temple Mound has turned up a significant amount of Late Archaic material, particularly pottery, and the pottery unearthed at Ocmulgee has allowed archaeologists to make some educated guesses about the arrival and settlement patterns of the people. Early pottery was designed with indirect heating in mind, with the heat usually provided by soapstone (steatite) slabs, while later pottery was tempered with fiber and could withstand direct heat. The first pottery objects at Ocmulgee tended to be quite plain, while more elaborate designs came later. Finally, direct heating vessels made of steatite itself became more common at the end of the Archaic period. The ceramic and lithic record seems to indicate that Late Archaic-era people moved into the Southeastern Plateau first, and then settled on the bluff near today's Funeral Mound. Though they traded with both coastal people and those further inland, they appear to have been more closely associated with inland communities through trade. Their use of stoneware and pottery indicates that they likely had a more diverse diet than earlier people, one that supplemented game and fish with soups, stews, and mast (a term that refers to various sorts of nuts and acorns).

OCMULGEE FIELD POEM

BIRD AND TURTLE

Tuckered out from running the trails,
the boy slows and takes the road back,
fingers laced together across his crown
so he can better breathe. He sees ripe
blackberries, bending their canes
over the stream. Though he loves them wild—
big as a thumb, blue as a gun, bleeding a tart,
deep purple from the risks they thrive in
(briars, chiggers, steep bank of creek), he
leaves them for the birds and turtles.
He passes on, tasting what he has not eaten.

*Oak shade takes him in. In the undergrowth
below the road's shoulder a stick snaps,
leaves shush: footsteps. He stops. Hunkers
down to glimpse through the leaves a brown flank,
a hind leg, stepping. Dead hunters inhabit
his stillness. It is their ghosts she comes to,
easing from the yearling trees, taking her own
turn to see, to flick one ear, then the other.
He hears the black molars of her hooves.
He feels honored to enter her regard.
She sniffs and is gone, as never there
as a leapt fish dropped back in the sea.
In a second, he will remember to breathe.*

OCMULGEE'S WOODLAND ERA

Like "Paleoindian" and "Archaic," "Woodland" is a term that came into being in the twentieth century. It can be used to refer to a region as vast as the eastern half of North America, and it can be used to refer to a lengthy span of time, roughly 3,000 years ago to 1,000 years ago. As hinted at above, for a long time, societies were classified as Woodland if they made pottery, lived in permanent villages, constructed some monumental architecture, and began to cultivate crops. But people had been doing these things in some places, including Ocmulgee, for centuries prior to the "official" beginning of the Woodland period. It is appropriate to use terms like Woodland, but we also must recognize that it is an imperfect shorthand that risks robbing the past of some of its complexity. Like the other periods discussed in this chapter, specialists further subdivide the Woodland into early, middle, and late. Early Woodland is usually characterized by the widespread adoption of pottery. Indeed, the Woodland period overall is associated with an astonishing array of pottery forms and styles. Middle Woodland societies began a long tradition of mound building, exchanged prestige goods regionally, and in some locales, began to grow maize. Late Woodland peoples intensified the production of corn and also began to fight using bows and arrows. Many of these developments can be seen in and around Ocmulgee, though their effects were not spread evenly over the entire region.

There are a number of important Woodland-era sites around Middle Georgia, including some on the Macon Plateau, Mossy Oak, and one of the most significant archaeological finds of the 1930s: Swift Creek. Middle Georgia has added immensely to our understanding of Woodland period life. Though later eras outweigh the Woodland in terms of sheer numbers of artifacts, the diversity of Woodland styles present in and around Ocmulgee is astounding. While Archaic-era pottery, when it was tempered at all, tended to be tempered with fiber, Woodland-era potters were more likely to mix their clay with grit or sand, which made for a more durable, heat-tolerant vessel. Early Woodland potters, such as those laboring in the Dunlap Fabric style (namesakes of today's Dunlap House and owners of part of the land that became Ocmulgee National Monument) sometimes impressed cloth or basketry into the wet clay to decorate their vessels. Middle and Late Woodland potters working in Middle Georgia elaborated on these traditions by stamping their wares with intricately carved wooden paddles or marking them with cords.

Swift Creek lies a few miles to the southeast of Ocmulgee National Monument. Arthur Kelly directed the excavation of the site and its mound in 1936 and 1937. Mound A, as he termed it, was about ten feet tall and 200 feet in diameter. It was likely constructed in stages around 500 CE, though perhaps not as rigorously planned as Mississippian-era mounds. Similarly, postholes on the mound indicated that

SWIFT CREEK Arthur Kelly first identified the Swift Creek pottery style near Macon in the 1930s. Many Swift Creek pots feature highly stylized natural patterns, which potters achieved by pressing a wooden paddle into the clay. (Photos by Susan Jennings and Gordon Johnston from the collection of Ocmulgee National Monument.)

structures of some kind once stood atop it, though those are not as regularly ordered as the buildings known to have stood on Mississippian-era mounds. The number of motifs present in Swift Creek Complicated Stamped pottery is stunning: stars inside circles, winged circles, interconnected spirals, and the like grace the outer walls of the pots. Once scholars in Middle Georgia identified this distinctive pottery style, their colleagues began to recognize it along a wide arc from northwestern Florida to Tennessee to South Carolina. It should not be assumed that Swift Creek people conquered their neighbors and imposed a new style regime. It is more likely that a diverse group of Native Southeasterners shared an iconographic language and set of technologies, cultivated food crops like squash and sunflowers in addition to gathering wild food and harvesting game, and traded valuable goods over long distances. Also, while we know from later historical and archaeological evidence that Mississippian-era societies were highly stratified, Swift Creek people throughout Middle Georgia lived in more egalitarian communities. One of the enduring mysteries of Ocmulgee is how the Late Woodland-era people who lived at the site interacted with their neighbors and how someone, whether an outside group or a native faction, remade Ocmulgee along Mississippian lines.

OCMULGEE FIELD NOTE

SEEING THE PLACE BREATHE

September 2016

Listening and looking at the mounds, the woods, the creek, and the river, at the open fields and wetland, you will begin, after a year or two, to see the place breathe. It will draw in one set of blooms, blossoms, and creatures and it will push out another. The sky will swell with the calling and circling of hawks in the fall, then they will be gone, passing like a wind on to another home. Around March, every field of short grass will hop with male robins in waistcoats the same color as a worn rubber basketball. In their time to, the maples will blow a long, gradual flare of gold, the cicadas will zither, mate, and clatter melodramatically as they die, and the bluegill will build their pebble beds in shallow eddies and butt anything that approaches. The waves of color crossing the groves of trees, the succession of blooms, the movement of animals and insects into and out of this borough of the watershed are an epic respiration. Each breath, measured in months, sends life out the arterial aquifers and streams and webs of roots. Each breath draws into busy graves the nourishing dead. The breath is expansive—one lung an ocean—but not one mote is wasted. Once you see it, you will know you're involved in its motion. You will detect it by the way it brings like lives together for mating and nursery-keeping and migration. It may make you crave kinship, a winter place to walk to with a herd of friends. It will remind you of your own breath and the lives that hang on it. The unseen air drawn in, pushed out. The invisible fire that keeps the world going. The voice, basso profundo, too deep-winded for human hearing, that sounds out every motion You will feel yourself in motion with everything else, riding the tide.

PART 3

MAKING MONUMENTS

In November 1828, Myron Bartlett, the editor of the *Macon Telegraph*, reported the sale of the "Reserve Land" and its "Ancient Mounds" on the east side of the Ocmulgee River. He wrote that the earthworks had "long been objects of curiosity to visitors and travelers, and furnished pleasant excursions to our village fashionables," but admitted that "we know nothing of their origin, or their history." After noting that some ridges and other features resembled coral, and reflecting on some marks that showed the "action of the sea," Bartlett concluded that the massive Ocmulgee mounds were probably "the work of Nature." Bartlett was far from correct in his conclusion, but he was far from alone. As the United States consolidated its rule over Native North America, its citizens came across monumental architecture of various sorts, and they struggled to reconcile such antiquity and grandeur with their limited understanding of human history and Native American culture. Wild theories abounded about the origins of the mounds, and during Bartlett's time, and for decades afterward, one of the most prevalent assumed the presence of a race of "Moundbuilders": civilized sophisticates, probably light-complexioned (of course!), who built on a grand scale. This noble race had since been defeated by supposedly savage and degraded Native Americans. Or perhaps a

Lost Tribe of Israelites made their way from the Middle East to North America. To the purveyors of these theories, Native people were inherently incapable of conceiving and executing monumental construction projects. Put bluntly, as Americans seized Native Americans' land, robbing peoples of their futures, they attempted to deny them their pasts as well.

We know how the mounds were built. Human hands scooped river-bottom clay into baskets. Human backs supported the heavy burdens, and human legs carried each load up the ramp to its spot at the flat top of the mound. Immense amounts of ingenuity and labor went into the construction of the earthworks. The story of why the mounds that dot the Southeast and Midwest were built is a little more complicated, and the story of who, precisely, built Ocmulgee has vexed non-Native historians and archaeologists from the infancy of their modern professions. Still, it has become something of a cliché to point out that the origins of the people who built the mounds and the purposes for which they were built are "shrouded in mystery," or some such. The film for sale at the visitor center carries the subtitle "Mysteries of the Mounds," for example. It's true we don't know all there is to know about the monumental architecture at Ocmulgee, and never will, but we know more than previous generations, and much of this new knowledge is the result of a fruitful collaboration between modern archaeologists and historians, Native and non-Native alike, and contemporary Native American communities.

MISSISSIPPIANISM ARRIVES AT THE MACON PLATEAU

In his 1956 handbook, Gus Pope speculated that the people who built the mounds were migrants from the confluence of the Missouri and Mississippi rivers by way of northeastern Tennessee. These "Master Farmers" effectively displaced, perhaps even conquered, the community that had settled at Ocmulgee previously, and proceeded to dominate life on the Macon Plateau for decades before their abrupt disappearance. In painting this picture, Pope relied on a set of ideas very much in vogue among archaeologists at the time. Human societies were ranked from simple to complex (or primitive to advanced, to use the language earlier generations would have), and the presence of agriculture was one of the markers of complexity. A large, prosperous, "advanced" farming society arriving from a neighboring region could not possibly coexist with people living under more "primitive" circumstances, and something would have to give. Archaeologists used the term "site unit

CAHOKIA Mississippian culture took shape between 700 and 900 along the Mississippi River between present-day St. Louis, Missouri, and Vicksburg, Mississippi. Perhaps its greatest culmination was Cahokia, where the Mississippi and Missouri Rivers meet in a rich bottomland. The largest, most densely populated site in North America in its time, its five and a half square miles plus suburbs was home to an estimated population of 38,000. From Cahokia, Mississippian culture spread southeastward and southwestward along river systems. (Painting by William Iseminger, Courtesy of Cahokia Mounds State Historic Park.)

intrusion" to describe the process, and Ocmulgee was considered a model of the type. Recent findings have called much of the foregoing into question.

"Mississippian" has multiple meanings. It is a time period (roughly 1000 to 1600 CE), but it's also a broad designation bestowed by archaeologists on ancient societies that featured chiefly lineages, hierarchical social structures, platform mounds, and, usually, a rich and varied diet with corn agriculture at its heart. Since the first and largest of these societies emerged at Cahokia, near the Mississippi River in southern Illinois in the 900s CE (with a period of rapid growth around 1050), archaeologists use "Mississippian" as a shorthand for communities organized along roughly similar lines. Deep analysis of ceramics indicates some similarities between pottery styles in use in eastern Tennessee and Ocmulgee, so a case could be made for outside influence around the time Ocmulgee began to demonstrate Mississippian traits. But once outsider pottery styles and materials appeared at Ocmulgee, the people there did not incorporate them wholesale or immediately. This would seem to suggest that Mississippianism need not have spread by conquest. Small groups of Mississippians, even trading parties or missionaries, could have struck out from any number of older towns and come into contact with local populations at places like Ocmulgee. The indigenous groups could in turn adopt or adapt Mississippian technology, artistic ideas, religious beliefs, as well as social organization schemes and the like. This model allows for more complexity and diversity, and seems to jibe better with the evidence. Though early radiocarbon dating suggested that Mississippians had colonized Ocmulgee in the 900s engaged in a period of rapid construction and expansion right around 1000, more recent analysis leans toward the conclusion that the Macon Plateau was emerging as the center of a sizable polity no earlier than 1100. Ocmulgee's origins are not as mysterious (or mysteriously early) as they have been perceived to be in the past. Even so, fitting Ocmulgee into a larger Early Mississippian context does nothing to diminish its significance.

EARLY MISSISSIPPIAN LIFE ON THE MACON PLATEAU

The Early Mississippians and their local hosts focused most of their energy on the South Plateau, near the Great Temple Mound of park literature, in the town's early years. From this point, until the site was ultimately abandoned in 1200 or shortly thereafter, reasonably dense settlements spread toward what archaeologists would label the Middle and North Plateaus, and satellite villages and farms lay miles beyond the current park boundaries in multiple directions.

Then as now, visitors approaching a Mississippian town would be immediately struck by the appearance of the mounds, and that fact is not an accident. Mississippian-era people at Ocmulgee and elsewhere chose propitious sites for their towns, usually in the vicinity of rich fall-line resources, and then plotted their communities and monuments in ways that both drew power from the surroundings and projected power to the outside world. The Great Temple Mound, or early archaeologists' "Mound A" (many of the site's features got new names in an effort toward public outreach in the 1950s), is approximately 49 feet tall and 979 feet square at the base, but it stands on a naturally occurring rise of roughly the same height, making it appear much taller. Since Mississippian towns like that at Ocmulgee cleared surrounding land for food production and fuel, the mound's appearance would not have been obscured by trees when it was in use. Today, grass grows on the mound slopes, but in its heyday, it featured smooth clay sides, interrupted by ramps or staircases, and probably a colored clay top, accentuated by a short curb at its edge.

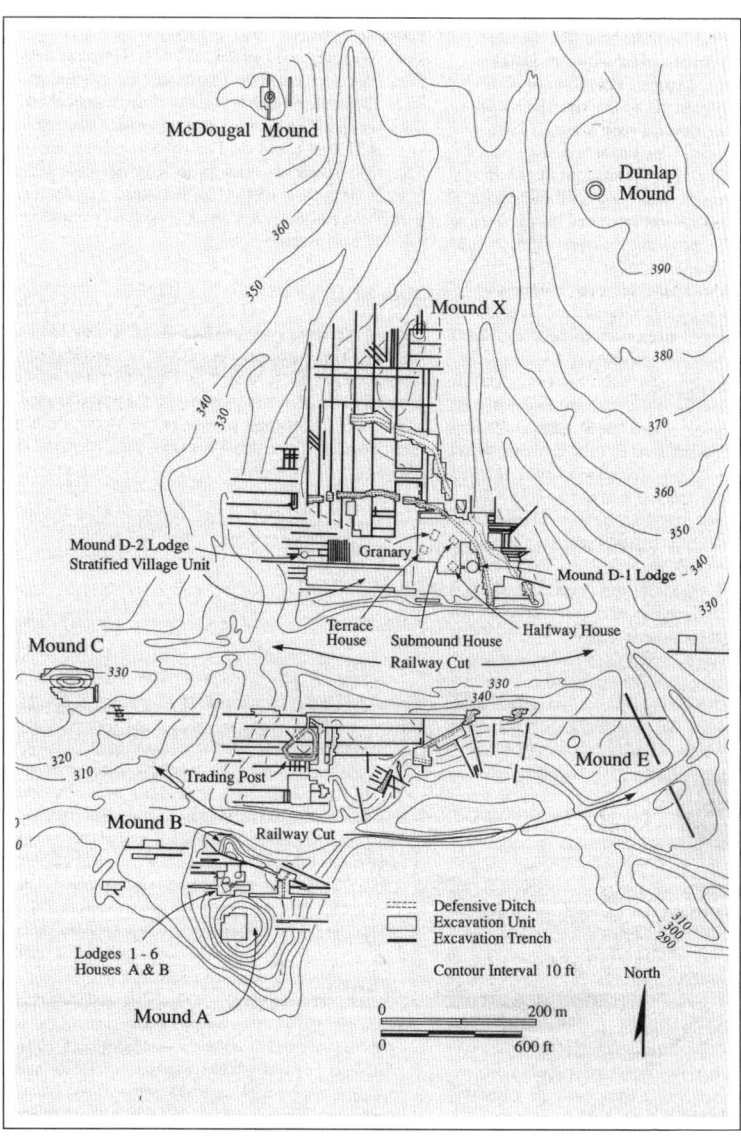

David Hally and Mark Williams compiled this striking topographical map of the Ocmulgee site for inclusion in Hally's 1994 *Ocmulgee Archaeology* volume. Note the alignment of the site's Mississippian features, the damage done by the railroad in the nineteenth century, and the twentieth-century archaeological trenches. (Used with permission of the University of Georgia Press. Copyright 1994 University of Georgia Press.)

GREAT TEMPLE MOUND Mississippian mound architecture both settled power in the land and projected power skyward. The Great Temple Mound was built on a natural rise one basketful of earth at a time. While in use, it was probably covered in smooth clay. (Courtesy National Park Service, Ocmulgee National Monument.)

Mississippians built mounds in stages, and it seems that at least four such stages comprised the construction of the Great Temple Mound. What prompted construction to start or stop is not clear, but perhaps when a significant leader died, priests ordered a new layer and the attendant destruction of moundtop buildings, or as a town grew in prestige, it added another stage. Many mounds had architecture on their summits, including ceremonial spaces and the residences of civil or religious elites, and, though Ocmulgee's largest mound has not been tested thoroughly, there is no reason to assume that it lacked these features. Indeed, the most recent archaeological work at the summit indicates a strong possibility of two paired structures on the eastern side of the platform at the penultimate stage of construction.

Most Mississippian towns featured large central plazas (Cahokia's was more than forty acres), and in many cases these central plazas were carefully constructed at around the same time, or even before, people built the mounds. Ocmulgee's settlement pattern and the disturbance of evidence in the intervening centuries make such a plaza difficult to discern in the archaeological record. One of Ocmulgee's striking features is the presence of clusters of dwellings across the Middle Plateau, and the apparent absence of a large, open ceremonial space at the town's core.

The planners of the Mississippian town at Ocmulgee envisioned and constructed several large-scale projects in these early waves of activity. Today these are known as the Lesser Temple Mound, the Funeral Mound, and the Earth Lodge, though these modern names may not match up precisely with their structures' early Mississippian-era functions or appearances.

Archaeologists labeled the ten-foot platform mound on the South Plateau "Mound B," though it was rechristened the Lesser Temple Mound in the mid-twentieth century, and it's notable for its proximity to the larger Great Temple Mound. Other Early Mississippian towns, such as the Toltec site in Arkansas, had multiple mounds, but they tended to be spread farther apart. Construction began on the Lesser Temple Mound around the same time that the Great Temple Mound was enlarged, suggesting that the town was expanding in both population and prestige. There were likely structures on top of the Lesser Temple Mound when it was in use, though archaeological investigations have been limited. This mound suffered extensive damage during the first episode of railroad construction, dating to the 1840s (more on this in part 5), and as a result, our ability to interpret the activities on its summit is limited. The Lesser Temple Mound may have been markedly larger immediately after it was built, too.

The Funeral Mound, or Mound C, was set aside, or consecrated, from an early date. While many Mississippian struc-

LESSER TEMPLE MOUND This classic image, with the Lesser Temple Mound on the left, shows the comparative sizes of the two mounds as they appeared in the mid-twentieth century. (Courtesy National Park Service, Ocmulgee National Monument.)

tures contained burials, Mound C's large number of human remains—150, from a variety of time periods—set it apart and inspired its current name. When it was first measured, in the 1870s, the Funeral Mound reached a height of thirty-nine feet, and this was in the aftermath of severe damage brought on by yet another railroad cut. Archaeological evidence indicates seven distinct stages of construction, several of which were capped with brightly colored clay. In fact, visitors to the early-twentieth-century excavation site were so awestruck by the colors that archaeologists commissioned an oil painting by Carolyn Meriwether to preserve the scene; they felt that schematic drawings and photography were inadequate. Even when rendered faithfully, "it may appear impossible that the mound mosaic should have been so brilliant as the painting indicates," archaeologist A. R. Kelly noted in a 1935 article for *Scientific American*. Today, the painting hangs in the museum's main corridor. The mound served as the final resting place for the early Mississippian-era elite, perhaps including the town's founders, who were entombed in a fashion befitting their high status, with prestige goods to accompany them. It is pos-

FUNERAL MOUND Archaeologist Arthur Kelly, who commissioned Carolyn Smith Meriwether to paint Mound C, described her as "a competent artist," and her painting as "both a scientific and an artistic record." Those who view the painting today would probably use more effusive language, especially after its cleaning in 2014. (Courtesy of Ocmulgee National Monument.)

sible that these high-ranking individuals were beneficiaries of double burials, once in a mound-top mortuary house, and subsequently in a grave inside the mound. Later occupants of the site also buried their dead in and around this mound.

As noted previously, the Mississippian settlement spread generally from south to north, and as the town approached the zenith of its power, construction began on a council house on the North Plateau, today's Earth Lodge. The process by which the Earth Lodge was excavated and preserved figures prominently in part 5, "Losing and Finding Ocmulgee." When it was in use, the council house boasted thick walls, the earth-embankment supports for which extended between thirteen and twenty-one feet from the chamber's interior. The chamber was nearly perfectly circular, with a forty-two-foot diameter. Four huge posts and a network of timbers supported a thatched roof with a smoke hole over a central fire pit. But the most

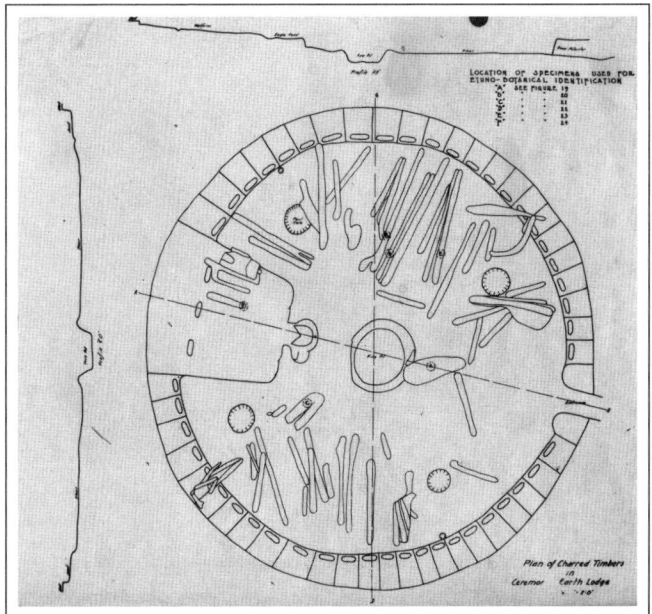

EARTH LODGE FLOOR This blueprint accentuates the effect of the eagle effigy and its forked eye, the central fire pit, and the four large posts that supported the roof. It also shows where charred timbers had fallen when the council house burned. (Courtesy National Park Service, Ocmulgee National Monument.)

remarkable feature, and one of the most remarkable examples of ancient Native American architecture overall, is the seating platform. Entering the earth lodge through the cramped passageway, as ancient guests would have done, it takes a moment for one's eyes to adjust to the dim interior. Directly across from the entrance is an effigy of a bird, probably an eagle or falcon with a forked eye motif, whose stylized body contains three prominent seats, and whose wings, spread elegantly along the chamber walls, provided individual seating for forty-seven more people. Twice yearly, the sun would shine through the entranceway and directly onto the platform party (today, trees, and the fact that the platform is sealed off to protect it, prevent the sunning and the sitting).

OCMULGEE FIELD NOTE

THE EARTH LODGE

October 22, 2013

Today—one of the two days each year the rising sun shines directly up the twenty-six-foot-long tunnel of the council house to light the raptor-shaped dais against its far wall—the overcast sky spits rain. The sun makes no real appearance until almost midmorning, so my hope of seeing the first gleam of sunrise strike the highest three seats in this old Mississippian meeting place is dashed, as it has been in earlier years. I settle for listening to the recorded voiceover in the lodge telling me the floor of the circular chamber is 998 years old, the chamber itself is within six inches of being a perfect circle, the pine trunk pillars supporting the roof are aligned north, south, east, and west, and the original entrance tunnel was twice as long and half as high as the current tunnel. Though the sun isn't cooperating today, the image of dawn penetrating a long, low tunnel to illuminate this raised falcon on the floor with his mysterious forked eye is vision enough to make me feel met. As I exit, I try to practice better seeing myself.

Outside, the spatter of rain has stopped. A long, horizontal rip of blue has opened to the east. The yellow and rust tones of fall give the undergrowth a dull glow, like embers. Due south, across the deep railroad cut, the Great Temple Mound stands flat-topped against the horizon. A billowing, vertical cloud, lighter than the gray sky behind it, seems to rest atop the mound like a fantastic hat. It feels like an invitation. I set off for the mound.

Crossing the footbridge over the railroad, I catch movement out of the corner of my eye: a whitetail canters away across the tracks below, then up the brushy bank of the cut maybe seventy yards away. I raise my binoculars, but it's too late. I move as quietly as I can over the bridge to the far bank, dialing in the binocs as I go in case the deer shows himself in the big field across from the old trading post site. Once I'm there, I see only sedge and shrubs. I'm disappointed, but I raise the field glasses to my eyes anyway.

The buck stands stock-still, facing me. The binocs have brought him so close my breath catches. We are eye-to-eye, gunfighting distance. He is fixed on me with penetration and focus—not like the hunted, but like the hunter. His neck is swollen with the rut, so that I feel as if I'm staring down a Division I offensive tackle. His rack is eight points for certain, maybe ten. He seems all one firm, fluid muscle. His hide is the precise color and visual texture of the undergrowth around him. After four minutes, he loses interest in me. I watch him for another quarter hour. When I move on, he only looks up briefly then goes back to browsing.

There are other sightings below the temple mounds and along the pond: three crows, strangely quiet and still, roost in the branches of a dead tree along the eastern shore. Nearby on a peeled gray trunk a woodpecker calls repeatedly until the crows drop one at a time off their branches and glide across the water. Five black-and-yellow spiders with leg-spans as wide as my hand hang centered in their webs. (If one of these scribbles your name in her web you're dead—so my grandfather told me.) In the web of the largest hangs, incredibly, an acorn as big as a grape, *caught mid-drop by spider silk I squint to perceive. On the path to the visitor center, another woodpecker hammers at a hole in the top of a snag. He isn't pecking rapid-fire. Rather, he rears back before each blow, deliberate, aiming, like a man axing notches into a log. The power in his neck and bill are the muscle of the buck scaled down.*

Coming out of the woods near my truck, I see that the rip of blue in the cloud cover has been stitched up. Not, I imagine, before a ray or two of light has pierced the tunnel and lit up the eye. At the truck, changing into my work shoes, I pull one foot out of a muddy boot. I let the toes wriggle for a second or two in the morning air before I push them into my wingtip.

* * * * *

Scholars debate how hierarchical Mississippian societies were, and the interpretation of the Ocmulgee Council House may have something to offer in this regard. For a long time, archaeologists and historians assumed that Mississippian polities were chiefdoms ruled by extraordinarily powerful individuals. Some certainly were, but "chiefdom" as a term is imprecise and biased toward a controversial (and widely criticized) model that assumes an evolution from band to tribe to chiefdom to state. Also, as archaeologist Timothy Pauketat has pointed out, if archaeologists look only for chiefdoms, that's all they'll find. The large number of seats in the council house might indicate a wider diffusion of power, or it might have been the place where lower-ranking individuals sought to curry the favor of higher-ranking ones. Simply put, we must allow for the possibility of a diversity of governmental forms among ancient Americans. Muskogee oral traditions indicate that the three special seats were reserved for a principal chief, second chief, and speaker, but we must be careful reading these traditions backward over centuries and across broad cultural divisions. (It's dangerous to assume linguistic, let alone cultural, affinity dating back a millennium, but the groups most closely associated with the legacy of Cahokia and its earliest heirs are Dhegiha Siouan speakers, such as Osages and Omahas.) The next chapter will examine the enduring Muskogee (Creek) connection to the site more fully. Radiocarbon dating tests carried out in the 1960s indicated that the Earth Lodge was built before about 1015 CE, with a margin of error of more than a century on either side, and destroyed by fire shortly thereafter. This seems extraordinarily early, and given the recent work by Daniel Bigman placing other artifacts from Ocmulgee's Early Mississippian flowering in a narrower and later window, from 1150 to 1210, it probably is too early to make sense.

Just to the west of the Earth Lodge lies Mound D, or the Cornfield Mound (named for a possible sub-mound field), a single-stage mound, six and a half feet tall, whose rectangular base covers an area of 11,000 or so square feet. Multiple buildings, three of which are labeled on early archaeological reports as the Granary, the Terrace House, and the Halfway House, are known to have existed on top of this low mound. So far this limited survey has treated just the monumental architecture within the first few decades of the site's expansion. Beyond the Cornfield Mound, the town planners laid out a defensive perimeter in the form of a ditch that might have also utilized some sections of palisade, but they appear to have abandoned work on it, started another one a little farther out, and abandoned that project as well. We will discuss the politics of the Early Mississippian period shortly, but it appears that at this time the ruling elite associated with the South Plateau (those who directed the construction of the Funeral Mound and the Temple Mounds) had reached the peak of its power and influence. Subsequent bursts of moundbuilding may illustrate a more diffuse pattern of governance. The construction of new mounds just north of the center of town (Mound X) and on the southeastern periphery (Mound E, or the Southeast Mound) would lend credence to this interpretation, as would the even later construction of Dunlap Mound, McDougal Mound, and possible Early Mississippian mounds near Fort Hawkins. Even though all were damaged significantly by later occupations, none of these projects seems as monumental or clearly articulated as the earlier structures.

OCMULGEE FIELD NOTE

BLUEBIRDS

June 8, 2013

I found myself between mounds—on my right the Great Temple, on my left the Lesser, which I realized I had never climbed in the daylight. Naturally, I ascended. I expected a view of the faded gray road running by below. What I got was the backs of flying bluebirds, seen from above. Bluebirds always merit admiration, but a thoroughly grounded, acrophobic man given a bird's eye view of a bird—the workings of the wings, the no-hands sleight-of-hand native to their veer and swoop, the dapper new denim dives and darts bush-to-bush across the washed-out asphalt—enters a place of grace. Their height of skill and precision, their weightless power, witnessed from a height greater than theirs, made breathing harder and better. For a second, it seemed the Mississippians had piled up their basketfuls of earth to raise this mound just so human eyes could see what I was seeing. The cryptic forked eye that is a common motif on ancient gorgets in that moment seemed simple—the visions of human being and bird joined in one staggering width and depth of field.

The bluebirds wove invisible nets, shooting like blue bullets from the high bank opposite me to the briers below me and back. One launched from a blackberry without the cane moving under him. What light touch was it? Whose light touch was it? He didn't know he did it. His hollow bones seemed holy. Ditto his coloring, his calling on the wing, the lacework under and the feathery overlay of his splendid person. Why, God, can't I fly in cursive?

But do bluebirds count? They are not self-conscious. They are denied the joy and burden of knowing their own beauty and skill, of reveling in it and knowing it as something that can be lost. Beyond that, each bird's holiness is hollowed out by the endless succession of eggs hatching—holiness ad infinitum. To what end? Endlessness?

The old Jewish story of creation implies that the great I AM in seeing that everything created was good doubted this opinion, or at least had to make an independent set of eyes with a certain distance and intellectual sense and wonder behind them with which to grasp at the tides, the trees, the intricacies of animal life, the firmament. We human beings are these eyes. We occupy the office of appreciator, of wonderer. But this hallowing isn't programmed into us. We don't boot into wonder at startup. Wonder is a capacity, not a reflex. Not even a tendency. Whether to cultivate it is the choice of the individual soul. There is also, of course, the capacity, just as uniquely human, for boredom—for a blindedness commensurate with familiarity and plenitude. An infinity of bluebirds is mundane. Then you fly above them, seeing the flow that brought these few here swooping through from others, these few from whom yet more will come, and it seems to signify. It gives God a name.

The Early Mississippian-era founders of Ocmulgee were clearly following a plan, though the ideology underlying the plan is difficult to discern. One student of the larger, earlier Mississippian city at Cahokia refers to that site as a "mirror of the cosmos," and this interpretation could apply to other such sites as well, even if the worldviews of the earliest Mississippians in the Southeast are hard to come by. The site might also have served as a "sociogram," in which a ranked social order was inscribed on the landscape, with the highest-ranking members living closest to the center (the Great and Lesser Temple Mounds) and restricting commoners' access to the sacred space around the Funeral Mound. Many Mississippian-era sites are oriented to the four cardinal directions, and Ocmulgee seems to conform to this pattern, more or less. The edges of the Great Temple Mound, though worn and rounded, face the north, south, east, and west, and the western edge aligns with the western edge of the Lesser Temple Mound. The individual features at Ocmulgee also demonstrate a kind of internal consistency, with structures facing each other across small courtyards, and the regular appearance of circular council houses (there are seven in all, and another at Brown's Mount) approximately 100 feet to the south or southeast of platform mounds.

Why mounds? The most obvious answer is that the people who built them came from areas where they were already widespread. There are also a handful of examples from earlier time periods (such as the Woodland-era mounds at Kolomoki, Swift Creek, and Cold Springs, a site on the Oconee River fifty-five miles north of Macon). The archaeological record provides some clues, and the early historical accounts do as well, but many modern Native nations descend from Mississippian roots, and these groups maintain their own diverse interpretations of mound architecture, and have for a long time, whether or not those interpretations were shared with non-Native settlers or academics. Since the connection between later inhabitants of Ocmulgee and modern tribes is clearer, we will discuss this issue again in a subsequent chapter. Some generalities are instructive, though. The heirs of the Mississippian world recognize the mounds as sites of great power, and, following their ancestors, associate them with some of the most fraught moments of life, such as birth or death. They are also sites of ritual purification and renewal. Multiple Native origin stories, including the Muskogee one treated at length in part 4 ("Sitting Down"), refer to monumental architecture.

OCMULGEE FIELD NOTE

AN EAR FOR EARTH

This morning, as I watched the morning sunlight drench the eastern face of the Great Temple Mound, I saw how the mound complements the site on which it was built. The swell of the land the mound is founded on makes it taller, more commanding. The generation of builders who began this earthwork raised it where there was already a rise. These builders came, they perceived what the earth was saying and doing, and they amplified it. The generations of people who succeeded those first builders continued the process, raising the mound one basketful of earth at a time. They helped the place say what it wanted. They did not, as we do now, make the place say what they wanted it to say.

The idea that a place could have something to say was not strange to them like it is to us, the people who have succeeded them here. The creation stories told by the Yuchis, Alabamas, Koasatis, and Cowetas—peoples who were important strands in what eventually wove itself into the tapestry that is now the Muskogee nation—all involve earth. The Alabamas and Koasatis tell of their earliest ancestors existing first underground and then emerging from a cave. Their oral stories tell where the cave is and how a root that blocked its mouth made some people Alabama and some Koasati. (The first tribe went around one side of the root and the second tribe went around the other.) The Yuchi, who appear to have been here earliest and longest, say they come from a drop of blood shed by the sun as it passed over the landscape. When the sun passed over again the next day, there where her blood had met the ground was a baby. The sun took the infant up and raised it into the first Yuchi. The earliest Muskogee, their stories say, came from earth to the West—a place considered the foundation or "backbone" of everything, likely the Rocky Mountains. In all these kindred peoples' stories, their ancestors came out of the ground. The earth said people. Knowing this, the people listen for what else the ground might say. Learning this from the people's stories, I try to listen with them.

Others do, too. Generations of people have tried to read the stories written in the mounds and the seven council houses at and around Ocmulgee and in other places where earlier people kept an ear to the ground. They have listened in their scientific way. Some have begun to learn a less scientific, more personal way of listening. This is humane. Though we listen in as many ways as we can, it will take many more sunrises to discern what the place is trying to say.

* * * * *

Most Mississippian-era people did not live on top of the mounds, of course, and the contours of their lives are somewhat more difficult to recover. Some of this difficulty is a result of 1930s archaeological practices. Archaeologists paid more attention to the grand monuments than to ordinary houses. Put another way, monumental architecture is important, but its very scale can sometimes skew our perceptions of Mississippian-era life. The 1930s uncovered the remains of several structures, and more recent surveys using sophisticated technology have filled in the picture somewhat, though much work remains to be done. Houses from the earliest period of the town's emergence on the South Plateau were circular with single post construction. As the town grew, its residents tended to build rectangular or square houses with wall trenches dug into to the ground, but they also tended to build houses of many different sizes, perhaps commensurate with a person's or lineage's status. All of these correspond to Mississippian-era house plans from other, more thoroughly excavated sites. In the space between the Great and Lesser Temple Mounds, strong evidence exists for a large rectangular structure (House A, for archaeology buffs), but it's not clear whether this was a public or private space. Round special-use buildings, perhaps sweat lodges or granaries, dotted the landscape nearby. Another group of square houses, sharing a courtyard and perhaps a round ceremonial space, graced the Middle Plateau. Still another abutted the Cornfield Mound.

It is not too much of a stretch to suggest, as we hinted earlier, that, beyond the residence of civil and religious leaders on top of the mounds, the highest-ranking family groups would live closest to the centers of power, and lower-ranking families would live farther afield. What to make of the rapid expansion of the town near the end of its occupation, then? Was this from natural increase or in-migration? How far did Early Mississippian influence at Ocmulgee reach? Can politics explain the rapid spread to Mound X, McDougal Mound, Southeast Mound, and Dunlap Mound? Was there a struggle for control that weakened the hold of those atop the

Great Temple Mound? Some of these questions are easier to propose answers to than others. The population at Ocmulgee, benefitting from rich resources and intensive agriculture, would likely have grown rapidly. Early Mississippian influence radiated out a few miles from Ocmulgee, though not nearly as far as, say, Cahokian influence would have. When neighboring communities saw the town's success, they may have sent emissaries or even migrated in groups, perhaps seeking the advantages of town life or military protection. Finally, there were tensions inherent in Mississippian-era governance as competing lineages—or even individual members of lineages—vied for control, so it's at least possible that the arrival of new families and clans could have introduced new wrinkles or exacerbated existing tensions, and the town dispersed. A remnant population likely continued to live at the site, but the Early Mississippian era of Ocmulgee history came to an abrupt end, probably in the early thirteenth century.

It is possible to reconstruct some details of Early Mississippian life at Ocmulgee pretty clearly. Not only do we have access to the artifacts unearthed here over the years, we can also consult data from other similar sites around the region. In addition to archaeological data, since some Mississippian polities were long-lived enough to enter into the documentary record, we can scour early travelers' accounts for information about Mississippian peoples. Finally, peoples descended from the Mississippians can, at times and in ways of their own choosing, allow outsiders insight into worldviews rooted in American antiquity.

Life in Mississippian-era Ocmulgee followed a seasonal cycle. In the spring, men would prepare fields for corn and squash (beans, the third of the so-called "Three Sisters" of Native agriculture, did not arrive in the region until the 1200s), but the actual planting and harvesting of crops was the province of women. Women also fashioned the pottery, used it to cook, and were primarily responsible for the care of children.

 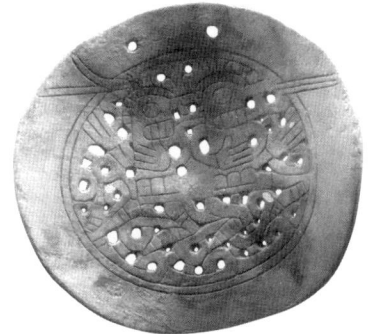

CHUNKEY STONE Carefully crafted stone discs (above left) were used in a game called chunkey. The game took place in a "chunkey yard"—a cleared stretch of ground bordered on two or more sides by earth banks. The chunkey stone (about two fingers wide and about two hand-breadths across) was rolled across this yard and male competitors threw a pole or stick, trying to strike closest to the spot where the stone would stop. Large bets were placed on the outcome. Many chunkey stones have been found at Mississippian sites and chunkey yards held a central place in Creek villages between the town house and the square ground. Native nations on the plains played tchung-kee with a hoop rather than a stone. (Photograph by Gordon Johnston from the collection of Ocmulgee National Monument.)

GORGET Gorgets, like the one shown to the right, were often made of marine shell and carved with elaborate stylized images and signified advanced social status. (Photograph by Gordon Johnston from the collection of Ocmulgee National Monument.)

People gathered wild food through much of the year, fruit in the summer and pecans and hickory nuts in the fall. In the spring, families would travel the short distance to the river to fish for catfish, gar, and turtles. Once the crops were harvested, men would travel slightly farther afield to hunt, often accompanied by their families. When a hunt was successful, the camp hummed with activity, as hides needed to be processed, fat had to be rendered into oil, and meat needed to be preserved. Thanks to the site's fall-line ecology, Ocmulgee's hunters had access to deer, as well as bears, raccoons, and a number of bird species. Water transport was vitally important to the people, and they expended great effort to fashion dugout canoes strong enough to guard against the river-bottom snags common to the region.

No one would mistake the Mississippian world for an earthly paradise. The polities that studded the ancient Southeast interacted with each other the way neighbors have throughout human history. They exchanged things of low value close to home and things of high value over greater distances. In addition to trade, they engaged in diplomacy and warfare as well. We should not assume that Mississippians were any more "warlike" than any other people, but warfare, as a way to gain manly prestige or enforce tributary status, was clearly an important part of Mississippian-era life on an individual and communal level. Witness the fact that the most prominent seats in the council house rest on the effigy of a bird of prey. Mississippians also celebrated women's roles in ways that baffled and upset early European observers. In addition to planting and harvesting fields, giving birth and raising children, women exercised political power, albeit in an indirect fashion. Mississippian societies were matrilineal, meaning that one's descent was reckoned through one's mother's line. Fathers were important, but a young Mississippian boy would learn his gender role from his maternal uncles. So, while women rarely served in positions of civil or religious authority, they influenced which men would hold those positions. These traits would continue well after the European invasion.

Ocmulgee, with a population around 2,000 and a reach of just a few miles, was probably not a particularly large or complex polity, so the number of lineages competing for influence was probably not that high. Competition could break out between individual members of a lineage, though, so the potential for governmental instability was ever present. Perhaps the geographic spread of the site discussed above was the outgrowth of such a rivalry. We know from later manifestations of Mississippianism that the male leaders of towns were often associated with the sun and creatures of the sky (such as the bird effigy on the Earth Lodge floor), whereas women's power tended to be associated with more earthly sources. The leaders of Mississippian towns combined religious, civil and military roles, sometimes in the same person, though more often different lineages were associated with some particular aspect of governance.

Some elements of Mississippian culture, like matrilineality, were so deeply seated that they survived well into the era of European colonization. Some even survive to the present. Two of these, Green Corn ceremonies and the manufacture and use of Black Drink, receive in-depth treatment in the next chapter. We know from a variety of sources that Mississippians conceived of the cosmos as a three-layered structure. The Upper World, associated with the sun, the sky, and its creatures (birds as well as supernatural beings), was an orderly realm. The Below World, a watery world, was more unpredictable, though also associated with fertility. This World hung in the balance between the two, sharing some aspects of each.

Mississippian-era art reflected the practical needs as well as the ideas and aesthetic concerns of the people who created it, and a similar iconographic language appears over large swaths of the South covering a long period of time (with some variation, of course): birdlike warriors, crosses, circles,

Jack Johnson drew this representation of the Mississippian worldview early in the twenty-first century. Mississippians posited the existence of Upper and Lower Worlds, with This World striking the balance in between. (Used with permission of F. Kent Reilly.)

BI-LOBED ARROW The bi-lobed arrow was a common motif (depicted above in the headdress) in Mississippian art, and often represented a combination of a bow and arrow, or perhaps in some cases a ceremonial pipe. This example, which hung in a gallery at Ocmulgee for decades, is based on copper plates from the Etowah site, a Mississippian town in northern Georgia. (Photograph by Matthew Jennings from the collection of Ocmulgee National Monument.)

HUMAN EFFIGY BOTTLE STOPPER The coloring, scale, and humanity of this bottle stopper in the form of a boy's head have charmed visitors to the Ocmulgee National Monument Visitor's Center for years, making it one of the site's most admired and recognizable artifacts. The stopper is hollow, with an opening in the back, perhaps allowing for the pouring out of water or other liquids. "Bottle Boy" is also the inspiration behind the Ocmulgee Field Note entries narrated from the perspective of boys. (Photograph by Gordon Johnston from the collection of Ocmulgee National Monument)

effigies both animal and human, to name just a few. Not every Mississippian town contains examples of every icon, but there's enough affinity that earlier generations of scholars posited the existence of a Southern Cult (a region-wide belief system) or a Southeastern Ceremonial Complex. At Ocmulgee,

MASTER FARMER
This "Master Farmer" (Mississippian) mannequin wears a magnificent headpiece made of panther jaws and sun-like copper discs befitting a man of high rank. (Postcard from Matthew Jennings's collection.)

FALCON EFFIGY PIPE This stone pipe demonstrates the fine carving skills of its maker. Birds of prey aroused great respect among the people native to Ocmulgee, who admired raptors' keen eyesight and their command of the sky—the Upper World. Tobacco was important in Native ceremonies and was often smoked in pipes rendered as animals. (National Park Service, Ocmulgee National Monument.)

apart from the council house floor, this can be seen in a headpiece unearthed at the Funeral Mound, which features a split set of copper-covered puma mandibles flanked on either side by finely wrought copper disks bearing a pattern reminiscent of the sun's rays. Stone pipes in the shapes of a falcon and a puma, smoothly polished chunkey stones (chunkey was a game played by young men in preparation for war and was an opportunity for community-wide gambling), and stone celts (axe-like tools), as well as a bottle stopper with a young boy's effigy atop it are other standout pieces.

Multiple styles of pottery have been unearthed at Ocmulgee, and the evolution of styles combined with the preference for one style over another have added substantially to our ability to reconstruct the site's history. Middle Georgia had pottery traditions reaching back hundreds of years. By the late Woodland period, many pieces adhered to the Vining

BIBB PLAIN POTTERY Mississippian pottery was made in a startling array of forms and styles and could be plain, brushed, cord-marked, or incised. Pots were coiled rather than turned on a wheel. The potter would wind a rope of clay atop a flat lap-board, then she would smooth and thin the walls of the vessel with moistened fingers. Once it dried, she would decorate it, then bury it in hot coals to fire. Water seeped through the walls of these unglazed pots, cooling what was inside. (Photograph by Matthew Jennings from the collection of Ocmulgee National Monument.)

Simple Stamped pattern, tempered by sand and decorated by pressing a paddle wrapped with string into the still-wet clay. Even after Mississippianism brought a new style, Bibb Plain, to the fore, Vining Simple Stamped did not disappear immediately or entirely. This is another piece of evidence to support the argument that the arrival of Mississippianism did not necessarily entail conquest, but rather that multiple groups might have interacted in more peaceful ways.

LATE MISSISSIPPIANISM AT LAMAR

One of the hallmarks of Mississippian-era life is the reoccupation or at least ceremonial reuse of sites, so it is strange that when a new group arrived around 1350, probably a community of eastward-migrating Hitchiti speakers (a member of the large family of Muskogean languages that also includes Chickasaw, Choctaw, and Muskogee/Creek), they chose not to reoccupy the Macon Plateau site and instead established a town a couple of miles south. Incidentally, there was an outpost of the Early Mississippian town there, but nothing like the massive earthworks that make up the current main park unit. Today, this site bears the name of the family that owned the land in later times: Lamar. As of this writing, access to the Lamar site is limited (archaeologist Mark Williams refers to it as a "thick hardwood and privet floodplain jungle filled with snakes and poison ivy"), but if and when the park expands, there are a number of intriguing interpretive possibilities associated with Lamar. Even when Lamar was accessible in the fourteenth through sixteenth centuries, it existed on a small rise of dry land surrounded by flood-prone areas unlikely to support intensive agriculture. Perhaps the Late Mississippians at the site exacted food and firewood tribute from their neighbors. Perhaps Lamar was not so much a province as a small elite compound (the town at Ocmulgee is generally reckoned at 173 acres, while just 21 acres are inside the palisade at Lamar). The architectural features of the Lamar site are striking. There are two large mounds, termed Mound A and Mound B, aligned on an east-west axis and separated by what *may* have been a small plaza. Comparatively limited archaeological excavations, compounded by discrepancies in archaeologists' reports, have left us with a fragmentary understanding of the Lamar site. Mound A is a truncated pyramid about twenty feet tall, with what appears to be a collapsed council house or earth lodge on its summit, and Mound B is a rounded mound, featuring a spiral ramp to the summit. Some park literature suggests that Mound B is unique, and that may be technically true, with a couple of caveats. The Rembert site, another Late Mississippian town in Elbert County, now beneath the waters of the Clark Hill Reservoir, had a similar mound. Second, it's at least possible that Mound B was never finished, and that the spiral ramp could have been filled in as the mound neared completion. Because of the early date of its excavation, "Lamar" would become a shorthand for other similar sites around the Southeast. Lamar's influence can also be seen today, since the frieze of the museum mimics the patterns around the rims of Lamar Bold Incised pots. The descendants of the people who built the Lamar mounds, who referred to themselves as Ichisi (possibly a Spanish-inflected

LAMAR SITE The Lamar Site, shown here in a twentieth-century aerial photograph, postdated the town on the Macon Plateau by two centuries and survived into the era of the European invasion. Hernando de Soto's army probably visited the site around Easter, 1540, erecting a cross on one of its mounds. Lamar is home to a rare spiral mound. (Courtesy of National Park Service, Ocmulgee National Monument.)

LAMAR BOLD INCISED POTTERY This pottery style features vivid lines and geometric patterns. This style of pottery was also the inspiration for some of the architectural details of the Visitor Center. (Courtesy of National Park Service, Ocmulgee National Monument.)

variant on Hitchiti, a language of the large Muskogean family, though this is difficult to prove), stayed in the area at least until the sixteenth century. By that time, they seem to have owed tribute to Ocute, a powerful polity on the Oconee River. As discussed in part 4, this may explain why they weren't immediately hostile to the heavily armed strangers who appeared in their midst in spring 1540.

These strangers from Europe by way of the Caribbean both witnessed and accelerated the dispersal of Mississippian polities. Of most pressing concern here is the *entrada* led by Hernando de Soto, who alternately stormed and stumbled through the Native Southeast in the sixteenth century. The *entrada* and its aftershocks inaugurated a process that would shake the Native Southeast to its foundations.

OCMULGEE FIELD NOTE

NOTE FROM A MOTEL NEAR ROME, GEORGIA

March 2017

The motor lodge I have just spent the night in has been built on a patch of level ground carved from the top of a hillside. As I eat my continental breakfast, there is something familiar about the view out the motel's glass wall. Beyond the pool, the morning sunlight washes over the broken ridge where it has been bulldozed and blasted. The field of scree at the base of the slope gleams with such a variety of rusts, pinks, and red-tinged whites that they lure me outside to see the hillside up close.

I'm more than a hundred miles from Ocmulgee National Monument, but the layers of color exposed here seem exactly those of the park's excavated funeral mound as it was painted in cross-section by Carolyn Smith Meriwether in 1933.

Yesterday's rain still saturates the clay and sand that have slurried from the pines crowning the hill to pile up here behind the motel. The ground gives with moisture under my boots. The rain is percolating down through the ridge on its gradual journey (down slope to stream or aquifer, from there to river and on to the ocean where it came from).

My first step off level ground and up the base of the slope is onto drier ground scattered with broken rocks. They are hard, angular, sharp with clefts. Each is its own microcosm of geology and tectonics, ribboned and faceted with color. A white seam of what looks like quartz runs through a russet chunk as big as my fist. The fourth rock I raise has flat faces and sheer edges on three sides. I'm pretty sure it's chert. If it were baked for the right length of time, a sequence of precise taps with a round hammer stone in a skilled hand would flake its facets into sharp, thin blades surgical enough to lay open game. Blades of it knapped into points with an antler butt would notch admirably into a length of river cane, yielding an arrow apt to pierce a deer or, if fired from a strong bow of Osage orange, the chainmail of one of Hernando de Soto's soldiers.

I'm due to hit the road and travel on, but for the moment the human and natural histories that meet here below the ridgetop, neither separable from the other, hold me in place. A culture grew from human responses to this landscape—to uses made of its varieties of wood, earth, rock, and animal life, uses that grew out of an abiding, unwritten knowledge of the landscape. Soon I'll be flashing through the Chattahoochee River valley at seventy miles per hour, but for another few minutes I feel the weight and the wealth of the chert in my hand and try to honor it. For now, I am grounded.

PART 4

SITTING DOWN

The messengers sent from Ichisi to greet the Spanish were generous. They brought gifts of animal skins to the soldiers' camp, but they also wanted answers. "Who are you? What do you want? Where are you going?" The people of Ichisi were right to be wary. The Spanish had announced their presence at the edge of Ichisi territory days earlier by seizing a handful of women and men, causing others to dive into the river to avoid capture, and helping themselves to the venison and turkeys that terrified towns people had left abandoned on their *barbacoa* (a word the Spanish borrowed from Arawaks to describe a frame of sticks used to roast meat over a low fire).

There are two versions of the Spanish response, delivered by Hernando de Soto through his translator Perico. In one, Soto said that he was "a Captain of the Great King of Spain," that he "came to give them to understand the sacred faith of Christ," and that if they would recognize these facts and place themselves under Spanish authority he "would treat them all well." In another, Soto replied that he was a "son of the sun and came from where it dwelt ... seeking the greatest lord and the richest province ...." After hosting Soto in the capital at Lamar for a single day, Ichisi directed the Spanish army eastward to Ocute, a larger town on the Oconee River.

This act of political savvy may have spared Ichisi the violence visited on other towns by Soto's army.

OCMULGEE FIELD NOTE

EASTER SUNDAY, 1540

Hernando de Soto, who has been a soldier since his teens, sits his armored horse and points toward the rough pine cross three of his halberdiers have spent the morning erecting atop the mound near the center of the fenced-in village. In the same thunderous Spanish he used to confront the Inca emperor years before as one of Cortez's officers, Soto tells the Micco and his people that he is the son of the sun and that this cross is the cross of the one true God, a power higher even than he, Soto. The people must revere this cross daily.

As Soto speaks, Juan Ortiz translates. For twelve years, Ortiz had been a slave of the Timucuan living along the Gulf of Mexico until Soto's men freed him nine months ago. Ortiz still quakes inwardly when Soto raises his voice at an Indian. Slavery leaves its shadow on a soul. The Micco has only one eye. Still, Ortiz can't meet his gaze.

As Ortiz speaks, the villagers bow and kneel as instructed, doing exactly as they have seen Soto's monks do. Ortiz feels his usual amazement at their obedience. Again gratitude swells at the base of his throat—relief at having, if not freedom exactly, a little choice, a little protection. The gratefulness—what truer form of grace and resurrection can there be than this that has been granted to him—makes him kneel and cross himself. His arm still remembers the motion, but after his long captivity it feels strange.

The sign of the cross ripples through Soto's other men as well. The gesture is a comfort in this deep swamp rich with alligators and serpents, inside this circle of high, sharpened stakes among people of naked muscle. The natives' bodies ripple with tattooed images of wild animals and strange symbols—completely different from the chaste white muslin mantles the women among the Micco's emissaries had worn when they had come out to meet Soto yesterday. Ortiz himself is scrolled with these native signs. He feels the other men staring at them when he sheds his borrowed clothes. He would like a shirt of that white muslin cloth. White is the natives' color of peace.

Ortiz can feel no peace inside the pickets that fortify this village. Unlike Soto's other men, Ortiz knows what losing a battle to people like the ones gathered between the two mounds means. His body bears the healed burns of his execution, which was stopped by the pleading of his captor's daughters, who had pitied his screams and intervened. That was years ago and a different people. Still, Ortiz is eager to be gone.

The Micco's words that Ortiz translated earlier today pointed Soto toward a river beyond the swollen one that they are close to now and that they have already crossed twice. Ortiz thinks about Benito Fernandez, the officer who had straggled at the back of the line and who as a result had drowned in one of the crossings. It had been on Maundy Thursday. He had sunk to the bottom under the weight of his armor after slipping off a footlog. Fernandez had died on his back like a flipped turtle, killed by his protection.

Though he wears Spanish clothes, Ortiz often feels he, too, could be killed by his protection. Soto's war dogs growl at him as they do at the Indians. The other men's eyes narrow in suspicion when Ortiz pairs Spanish subjects with Indian verbs.

Ortiz would like to be farther from Benito's grave and farther still from this pen of giant spears. He watches Soto sitting his horse. When Ortiz sees the son of the sun turn his hard face to the Micco, he tries to steel himself. He knows Soto is about to thunder again.

"I accept the food you offer. You will give me burden-bearers to carry it along the path to this Ocute you speak of."

Soto does not look away from the Micco's face as Ortiz translates his order and the Micco's contrition. They will move on today. Ortiz feels his spirits rise. He won't feel such relief again for almost two years—until, inside a similar palisade that the army will build for its winter camp—he dies.

MISSISSIPPIAN DISPERSAL

The scope of the changes that brought the Late Mississippian and Spanish colonial worlds together at the Lamar site in spring 1540 is too vast to cover fully here. Library shelves groan under the burden of the annals of the so-called Age of Discovery. But in another sense, we need not concern ourselves too much with the rise of merchant capitalism (one recent interpretation calls it "war capitalism") and militant Christianity in Europe, the leading role of Castile in the centuries-long conflict with Muslims in Iberia, and the subsequent push across the Atlantic.

If we keep a tight focus on Late Mississippian-era Ocmulgee, we see that the Mississippians and Spaniards who met in 1540 had a lot in common. In addition to their obvious shared humanity, both groups had highly articulated systems of rank and sophisticated military cultures. While the sudden appearance of the Spanish was probably not welcome, Ichisi dealt with the problem as they would have with any group of heavily armed outsiders with a proven capacity for avarice and violence. They aimed them at their neighbors in Ocute, perhaps in hopes of weakening that polity. Then they went about their lives.

But life in the Mississippian Southeast was changing. These changes had their roots not only in a changing environment but also in the network of political agreements that held the Mississippian world together. A prolonged period of warming coincided with Mississippianism's early florescence. This Medieval Warm Period, which lasted from 800 to 1300 CE, allowed for the spread of agriculture and all its attendant effects. An episode dubbed "The Little Ice Age" followed, from the 1300s to the 1800s, and, in general, crop surpluses were more difficult to achieve and sustain. Ideally, a large Mississippian community would produce a year's surplus every year, to inure itself against a future crop failure. Periods of drought could accentuate food shortages and lead to the dispersal of centralized polities. Documentary evidence gleaned from the period just after Soto's *entrada*, in concert with climate data, indicates several such droughts. Some towns that had plenty of food to offer their unwelcome guests in the 1540s were struggling to feed their people in the 1550s, for example.

As alluded to in the last chapter, the political structures that undergirded Late Mississippian life could be unstable on both intra- and inter-town levels. Competing lineages within a town could foment factionalism and spin off new communities or weaken established leaders' authority. At the regional level, archaeologist David Anderson has described a process he terms "cycling." Competition between elites of neighboring towns could produce more complex chiefdoms, and competition between such polities could lead to the establishment of paramount centers, or fragmentation, or the former followed by the latter. When Soto arrived in Ichisi, that town was likely not a power player in the region but may have been tied in some way, perhaps in a tributary fashion, to the larger Ocute on the Oconee River. Ocute itself had been a paramount center in years past but appears to have been in decline by the 1540s.

Every schoolchild knows that Native Americans were decimated by European diseases to which they had no immunity, and this opened the door to the conquest of eastern North America. While this remains true to an extent, disease made inroads into Native communities in different times. The main epidemics that swept through the Southeast occurred in the late 1600s as a result of the Indian slave trade emanating from Charles Town (today's Charleston), the capital of English Carolina. We'll discuss this trade more extensively below. If epidemic disease was less important in the 1500s, Soto's army still disrupted what may have already been a tenuous food situation, and the disruption likely fragmented previously centralized towns. If leaders lost control of food surpluses, the repercussions could be wide-ranging and include civil unrest. There is clear evidence that Soto's army destabilized multiple polities as it tore through the Southeast, seizing food stores, playing off town against town and upsetting the balance of power, but we cannot say for certain that this was the case with the town at the Lamar site.

Hernando de Soto arrived in the Americas as a teenager in the 1510s, and subsequently distinguished himself in the Spanish invasions of Panama and Nicaragua. In the 1530s, he was a leading agent in the destruction of the Inca Empire. During these exploits, he also managed to cultivate a reputation for extraordinary violence, whether in the use of specially trained mastiffs and greyhounds to tear at Indian flesh, or in hunting people on horseback, or rendering the fat of his defeated enemies to caulk a boat. His army of 600 or so, attempting to replicate earlier Spanish successes in Peru and Mexico, came ashore at Tampa Bay in 1539 and proceeded to

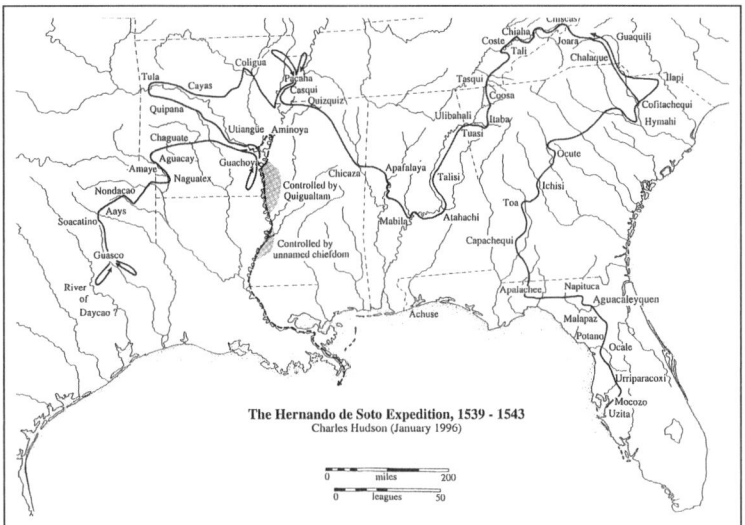

Painstaking work done by Charles Hudson resulted in this understanding of Soto's route through the Southeast. Though additional evidence may come to light, and this route is not without some controversy, it remains the most widely accepted interpretation. Soto did not survive the expedition he led, dying of fever along the Mississippi in May, 1542. His army, turned back from their journey westward by lack of food and by effective Native ambushes, eventually built boats and fled down the river to the Gulf Coast and Mexico, pursued much of the way by large canoes of Native warriors, possibly the ancestors of the Natchez. (Reprinted from *The Hernando de Soto Expedition: History, Historiography, and "Discovery" in the Southeast*, edited by Patricia Galloway, by permission of the University of Nebraska Press. Copyright 1997 by the University of Nebraska Press.)

wind its way from town to town. A closer look at the meeting of Ichisi and Spain can give us a clearer picture of the late Mississippian world in Middle Georgia.

After the exchange that opened this chapter, Soto's army proceeded to the capital of Ichisi, the palisaded mound complex at Lamar. Soto's secretary, Rodrigo Rangel, described the approach: "They arrived at the Great River, where they had many canoes in which they crossed very well and arrived at the town of the lord, who was one-eyed, and he gave them very good food and fifteen Indians to carry the burdens." Since the lord had sent peaceful emissaries, "they did not wish to be tiresome." On April 1, they erected a wooden "cross on the mound of the town and informed them through the interpreter of the sanctity of the cross." According to this account, the people of Ichisi were properly awed: "They received it and appeared to adore it with much devotion." Another account of the same incident, one associated with a soldier from the Portuguese town of Elvas, frames it in much the same way. Soto "left a wooden cross raised very high in the middle of the public place." After the Spanish explained the cross's meaning, they instructed their hosts to revere it, and "they signified that they would do so." In the twentieth century, Macon's civic boosters would commemorate this moment as the entrance of Christianity into the region. The reality was more complicated and less to crow about.

In the Spanish documents, we can see the layers of control exercised by even a minor regional leader. The "one-eyed lord" did not venture out of his town. Rather, upon hearing accounts of the Spanish presence, he sent some people of lower rank to greet the Spanish according to Mississippian diplomatic protocols. Whatever they told their leader, he allowed the army to proceed unhindered to the capital. Maybe they warned him of the Spanish armaments and he deemed the cost of resistance too great. Maybe he intended to turn the Spanish toward his rival or superior on the Oconee. Or perhaps it was a combination of all these factors that informed his behavior. We can glean some other clues about late Mississippian life from the brief accounts. Elites, and especially chiefs, held others as status symbols and sources of labor, and could gift their captives to others of like rank, as in when the lord of Ichisi gave Soto fifteen burden bearers. This version of slavery shares some aspects of other forms of bondage in later America, but it was a product of the Mississippian world and shouldn't be confused with more widely known forms of slavery, like that which drove nineteenth-century cotton production.

Mississippians practiced sharp diplomacy and employed systems of rank that relegated some people (perhaps captives from other towns) to the status of slave. Their apparently easy acceptance of Christianity is more difficult to explain. The elites of Ichisi may have been familiar with reports from other provinces that detailed Spanish violence and the practice of taking hostage both commoners and those of high status. They likely wanted Soto to leave. So they suffered the insult of the placement of the cross and a short lecture in order to maintain peace and send Soto's force on its way.

We also have to allow for the fact that the Spanish used Christianity, and Native peoples' lack of it, to legitimate their presence, and their behavior, in foreign lands, so if they could report Native willingness to convert, that might please their superiors and lead to support for future missions. As quickly as it appeared on the edge of Ichisi, the Spanish army marched off toward Ocute, and from there into a thinly populated "desert" in the Savannah River country, before ultimately turning north toward the mountains. Ultimately, Soto would not find a North American analogue to the wealthy lands of Mesoamerica and the Andes. He died in 1542 and received his own double burial of sorts, first in the ground and later at the bottom of the Mississippi River.

Since the 1560s *entradas* of Tristán de Luna y Arellano and Juan Pardo did not reach the Ocmulgee or the Oconee, the documentary evidence for Ichisi and Ocute is lacking. Archaeology can help fill in this gap in our historical knowledge, at least in part. Through tracing ceramic patterns, archaeologists note a spike in settlement along the Oconee contemporary with Soto's *entrada*, which might connect to Ocute's rise in prominence and the subsequent abandonment of all the mound centers on that river by the 1580s. Ichisi, unlike many other Lamar-era sites, had managed to sustain continuous occupation from the 1300s through the arrival of Europeans but appears to have been abandoned in the late sixteenth century. Though historical documents and the archaeological record are not definitive on such matters, it is safe to assume that remnant communities left over from the Macon Plateau and Ichisi did not abandon the region entirely. Rather, they left their ceremonial centers and reorganized their communities in ways that fit the changing times. Archaeologist John Worth has tied Ichisi and other dispersed Mississippian polities, Altamaha and Ocute, to the emergence of the Yamasee people in the seventeenth century. It should be obvious by now that the people were no strangers to change. In the distant past, their ancestors had adapted to their environments by constructing massive earthworks, palisades, and centralized governments. Native people would continue to adapt to the presence of outsiders in their homelands.

OCMULGEE, TRADE, AND CREEKS

Some of the marketing materials for Macon and Ocmulgee National Monument, including a large billboard on Interstate 75 as of this writing, tout 17,000 years of continuous human occupation. We've already seen that 17,000 is probably something of a stretch. In the interest of historical accuracy, it must be noted that *continuous* is probably a bit of an exaggeration, too. There are gaps in which it is impossible to say with certainty that either the main park unit or the Lamar site was inhabited, but neither can we say for certain that they weren't. People still lived in the area, but it is difficult to discern if their presence was continuous. By the late 1600s, there is indisputable documentary and archaeological proof that people again lived at Ocmulgee. It's also during this time that we have some idea of what the people who lived here called the site (some called it Ocmulgee!), and of the name bestowed on the area and its inhabitants by a new group of European outsiders (Ochese Creek and Ochese Creek Indians).

OCMULGEE FIELD NOTE

MIDDLING

The last people to make a home here along the Ocmulgee tell stories of passing through this place and then returning to it. They had to see the rest of the land—the hills and creek bottoms east of this river that led to another big, rocky stream and also the flatter, sandier forests directly downstream from here, where the river gave up its boulders and waterfalls to bend in sweeping turns around sandbars and to back up into swamps. They saw how this particular reach of this particular river could shelter and feed them better than other areas. They probably saw it as a middle—a place between shoals where fish could be caught in weirs and swamps where they could disappear when enemies came raiding, a ground both near enough to the river to make farming its moist bottomland easy and high enough that their homes would be safe when the river raged and flooded. The place also lay between the sea, to which the river carried everything, and the uplands. It was a crossroads where both the sought-after shells and salt gathered by the people who lived beside the ocean and the chert and clay gathered and worked by the people of the hills and mountains could be traded. The people who settled here appreciated middle places, and the river they came to call Ocmulgee had many appealing "middlenesses." They passed through, paying attention, then they returned to stay—to "sit down."

The people listened to the place in order to learn its names. The river shoaled noisily not far north, foaming and breaking in a rocky bed craggy with islands. Rain swelled it at times into a boiling, rushing torrent that gnawed its own banks and felled trees. What it did, it was—"bubbling waters" or "Ocmulgee." Its act was its name. This Muscogee word the people used when they told the story of re-arriving here with the intention to stay also refers to sitting down—and not sitting down for a short rest during a long journey or camping for a night on the way elsewhere, but sitting heavily, giving the people's full weight to the ground, trusting it to hold them up. Imagine the broad hips and backside of a sturdy woman—a matriarch in the ruddy, broadening bloom of her child-bearing years—against the earth. The plenty and potential of the people met the plenty and potential of the place cheek to cheek. This sitting down was not passive or inert. It was a setting out. The people began a journey in place. Their destination was belonging there. The people would become the place's.

As the place fed their bodies and grew their numbers, it also fed their spirit, their imagination, and their sense of who they were together. The earth here germinated stories and beliefs in the people as they germinated hills of corn, squash, and (later) beans in its rich river bottom. These crops they called the Three Sisters. Their community depended on these sisters, which grew bountifully and which could be stored. The growth of the sisters was inseparable from the growth of the community and so female, maternal power held a central place in the people's reverence. The women had stewardship and say-so over crop land, and every person's family identity was determined by who their mother and grandmothers were. There were male spheres of authority, too. The river was Long Man, a rangy, stringy, ropey-muscled meanderer with his head in the hills and his feet in the sea. Mothers left their tightly swaddled babies on his banks near waterfalls and chutes so the children would learn what Long Man had to teach. The river figured in many stories and his influence met and balanced female power in the people's stories.

The people depended on the animals of this place as well. In their stories, animals came down from the upper world to this one first. Crawfish after several failed dives finally brought up from the bottom of the original all-encompassing waters the dollop of mud that grew into the earth. The wing-strokes of the great birds carved the mud, drying it into ridges and creek bottoms. The water spider brought sacred fire in his web basket across the water from the island where lightning first brought it to earth. The acts of animals were acts of origination and power that made human life possible and better and that offer model qualities that human communities are called on to emulate. Superior animal powers of vision, quickness, and strength could be drawn into human use through the use of skins, feathers, and other revered animal parts.

The foundation under these lives that human life depended on and was braided into was the land itself—the watershed with its flowing river and rich dirt. The earth said deer, said corn and beans, said wattle-and-daub houses and frond roofs. The people listened and accepted the place's gifts and challenges. They submitted to the earth and let it shape and infer their definitions of health, wholeness, community, and sanctity. The mounds remind us that places speak. They remind us that human beings can choose to listen.

* * * * *

In the throes of the Little Ice Age and the aftermath of various Spanish incursions, larger Native polities throughout the Southeast dispersed. As they did so, they spun off numerous smaller communities, which, though they may have shared broad linguistic and cultural affinities, were not exactly the same and could influence each other through conflict or more benign contacts. Such a process likely occurred on the Alabama side of the Chattahoochee River in the 1500s and 1600s. Evidence indicates a general easterly migration on the part some of the descendants of Moundville, a large Mississippian town on the Black Warrior River and a southwesterly move on the part of some of the descendants of Etowah, another impressive mound center in North Georgia. These fused, pluralist societies combined with local elements to produce new fused, pluralist societies. We can be even more specific: during what archaeologists call the Blackmon Phase

OCMULGEE FIELDS INCISED POTTERY A bowl typical of the Ocmulgee Fields Incised style. Note the swirling energy and strength of the incisions and the thin walls of this basketball-sized vessel. (Photograph by Gordon Johnston from the collection of Courtesy Ocmulgee National Monument.)

(beginning in 1600), people along the Middle Chattahoochee combined coarse, sand-tempered, Etowah-derived pottery and shell-tempered pottery derived from distant predecessors at Moundville into a new type of ceramic, and they decorated the pots with lines, scrolls, and chevrons, then smoothed the markings somewhat. In the 1930s, when workers at Macon excavated piece after piece of it, archaeologists Jesse Jennings (no relation) and Charles Fairbanks christened it Ocmulgee Fields Incised. They mistakenly assumed that it had evolved out of Lamar in a local setting (Gus Pope, in his mid-twentieth-century handbook, followed this line of thinking and called the people at Lamar "Early Creeks"). Now scholars believe that it was one of a number of signals of a new presence on the Macon Plateau. These new arrivals were the heirs of centuries of cultural transformation, and, more recently, the survivors of an attack on their Chattahoochee towns, and they were the progenitors of one of the most powerful and durable Native nations in the South, and one crucially important to understanding Ocmulgee's history: the Muskogees.

OCMULGEE FIELD NOTE

SKY PEOPLE

(This story was told by Muscogee storyteller and flute-player William Harjo to approximately thirty young elementary school children and six adults at Ocmulgee National Monument on September 6, 2016, where it was recorded and transcribed by Ashlyn Rebel. Mr. Harjo first heard the story from Randy Miller, a Seminole Creek who

often told the story to children to cultivate imagination and wisdom in them.)

Okay, now, way back in the beginning— this is called Sky People. Before there was any land here, it was all nothing but water. And everybody had to live up in the sky. And the eagle was in charge of everything in the, you know, was in charge of all the Sky People. So one day he called everybody together and he told them, he said, "You know, we need to live on some land. So we need somebody to go down to Earth and find some land. Do I have any volunteers?" The eagle, he didn't get any volunteers at all. And so he kept saying, "I need someone to go down and see if they can find land." And as they were doing this, finally, way in the back of the room, this little animal didn't even have a hand. He had little pinchers. He stuck his hands up, like this, says, "I'll go! Mr. Eagle, I'll go! I'll go!" And what he was is, we call him a... where I grew up we call him crawfish; in Louisiana they call him crayfish. And, you know, it's that little thing that's got a crooked tail and he walks backwards and he's got pinchers... Anyway, he said he was going to jump down and find land. So the eagle gave him four days to find land. So he came out of the sky and he landed in the water and he swam to the north and he didn't find any land. He swam to the east and he didn't find any land. He swam to the south; he didn't find any land. He swam to the west; he didn't find any land anywhere. So his time was almost up and he says, "Now, I've swam every direction that I can, except one, and I'll have to try it." So he drew in a great, big, ol' breath and he went down and he started going underwater. And he kept trying and going and going and going and you know what, he ran into something soft at the bottom, and so he touched it and he started piling it on top of each other, like this, he kept piling all that and what it was was mud, he ran into the mud. So he kept *piling mud up until he brought it up out of the water. And then he came up and it was time for him to go back so he returned and reported back to the Sky Council and told the eagle, he says, "Well, did you find any land?" He says, "No, I did not find any land, but I found something really soft and wet we call mud." He says, "Okay, do you think if we were to dry it out, maybe we could live on it?" He says, "Well, maybe." So the eagle says, "Okay, now I need a volunteer for someone to go dry this mud out so we can live on it." The eagle he didn't get any volunteers. So he announced, he says, "I'll go down, and I'll try to dry all this land out." So that's what he did. He came out of the sky, and as he was flying over this, trying to dry it out, he started getting tired on the fourth day, and he was getting tired, and he had to push harder and harder with his wings to keep himself flying, so as he was doing that, he pushed all the mud back and that's how he created hills, and valleys, and mountains, so that's how come our land is the way it is today, from when the eagle came and dried everything up.*

* * * * *

After utterly annihilating two French outposts, the Spanish established St. Augustine in 1565, not so much to project power into the American interior as to protect valuable shipping lanes between wealthy Caribbean colonies and Spain. Also, starting in the 1560s, the Spanish founded dozens of missions. The earliest were Jesuit undertakings, but the Franciscans eventually dominated the field. Nearly a century after St. Augustine, in 1656, the Spanish founded San Luis de Talimali on the Gulf Coast site of present-day Tallahassee. Working north of San Luis, in the region drained by the Flint and the Chattahoochee, Spanish missionaries hoped to gain souls, Spanish traders hoped to turn profits, and Spanish diplomats and officials hoped to discourage other powers' imperial ambitions. This last point grew increasingly imperative when a fledgling English colony appeared on the horizon.

After his restoration to the English throne in 1660, Charles II was generous toward those who had supported him during his exile, among them Anthony Ashley Cooper, Earl of Shaftesbury. Shaftesbury and several associates, the Lords Proprietors, were granted a wide swath of land, from the bottom of Virginia to a point south of St. Augustine, and extending notionally to the Pacific, to administer as they saw fit. They saw fit to establish the colony of Carolina in 1670. The part of this story that matters most to Ocmulgee is the world of trading possibilities opened up by the English. In the simplest terms, the English operating out of Charles Town offered more desirable goods than the Spanish at more affordable prices.

In the 1680s, Henry Woodward, Carolina's Indian expert, sought to expand English trading influence in the interior Southeast. He traded, distributed presents, and apparently formed enough of a bond with the region's peoples that the Spanish sent an army out to catch him. Lieutenant Governor Antonio Mateos, with six Spanish soldiers and perhaps 200 armed Apalachees, set off to capture Dr. Woodward. Native informants tipped Woodward off, and he and other traders went into hiding, but he did manage to leave a note for his pursuers: "I trust in God that I shall meet you gentlemen later when I have a larger following." Mateos returned with a larger army in 1686. Woodward was back in Charles Town, so Mateos and his force vented their frustration on the symbols of the English presence, taking firearms and dressed skins. They burned the four towns they perceived to be closest to the English: Tuskegee, Kolomi (alternately Coolamee), Coweta, and Kasihta (alternately Cusseta). Though a representative of the towns went to the Spanish to prove their loyalty, and Mateos was recalled, the relationship was badly strained. In

1689, the Spanish attempted to reinforce their "control" over the province they called Apalachicola by building a fort near the town of Coweta on the Chattahoochee and demanding that the surrounding communities give up their trade with the English. This ham-fisted attempt to enforce a trade monopoly was the final straw for many people, who moved en masse to the Ocmulgee in late 1689 and early 1690. The Spanish demolished their fort, even pulling the few nails that were used in its construction and filling in its defensive trenches so no one else could make use of them.

For the next twenty-plus years, towns sprang to life on both sides of the Ocmulgee River, and the high land beside the ancient mounds buzzed with activity. Until the 1930s, references to the English trading post on the Ocmulgee were vague. Scholars knew there was one, and the Ocmulgee site was a strong candidate, based on Spanish and English documents. Excavations done in the 1930s and written up over the subsequent decades, most significantly by Carol Mason in the 1960s, have proven that the Ocmulgee site was a center of Anglo-Indian commerce. With these archaeological findings, historians have taken a new look at the documents, and a fuller picture of the site has been the result. In 2001, the National Park Service conducted new archaeological surveys in a recently gifted area of Ocmulgee, Drake's Field. These, as well as more recent work, have sketched the outline of a large Creek town (or towns) centered on the Middle Plateau near the Trading Post and stretching to the north and west to an as-yet-undetermined extent. Before we explore the basics of the settlement, we should listen to Muskogee voices explain their arrival on the Macon Plateau and attempt to disentangle some confusing nomenclature.

"If we are to give credit to the account the Creeks give of themselves," wrote William Bartram, "this place is remarkable for being the first town or settlement, when they sat down (as they term it) or established themselves, after their emigration from the west, beyond the Missisippi [sic], their original native country." Bartram visited Ocmulgee in July 1775 and again in January 1776. He described the site's appearance at that time before explaining its significance to at least one group of Creeks. Bartram noted that "On the heights of these low grounds are yet visible monuments, or traces, of an ancient town, such as artificial mounts or terraces, squares and banks, encircling considerable areas. Their old fields and planting land extend up and down the river, fifteen or twenty miles from this site." Bartram then relayed a Creek version of the events of the 1500s through the 1700s, which bears quoting at length:

> On this long journey they suffered great and innumerable difficulties, encountering and vanquishing numerous and valiant tribes of Indians, who opposed and retarded their march. Having crossed the river, still pushing eastward, they were obliged to make a stand, and fortify themselves in this place, as their only remaining hope, being to the last degree persecuted and weakened by their surrounding foes. Having formed for themselves this retreat, and driven off the inhabitants by degrees, they recovered their spirits, and again faced their enemies, when they came off victorious in a memorable and decisive battle. They afterwards gradually subdued their surrounding enemies, strengthening themselves by taking into confederacy the vanquished tribes.
> AND they say, also, that about this period the English were establishing the colony of Carolina, and the Creeks, understanding that they were a powerful, warlike people, sent deputies to Charleston, their capital, offering them their friendship and alliance, which was accepted, and, in consequence thereof, a treaty took place between them, which has remained inviolable to this day: they never ceased war against the numerous and potent bands of Indians, who then surrounded and cramped the English plantations... until they had extirpated them. The Yamasees and their

adherents sheltering themselves under the power and protection of the Spaniards of East Florida, they pursued them to the very gates of St. Augustine.

What are we to make of this rendering of Creek history? It is true that the Creeks traced their origins to the west, and that many of their origin stories include an epic migration. Beyond that vague sense of claiming Ocmulgee as a Creek homeland, the story also justifies the Creek presence in ways that the English would have understood: Ocmulgee is ours because we fought for it. Ultimately, the story combines older Muskogee origin stories with a glimpse into the way that one group of Creeks understood their more recent history, or rather wanted Bartram, and by extension the English colonists, to view that history. In this sense, the story should not be understood as a literal re-telling of Creek history, but as an argument designed to prove Kasihta's preeminence among Creek towns and Creek precedence in the region and to highlight moments of Anglo-Creek alliance (even if the story glosses over such incidents as the Yamasee War in the process). What Bartram relayed was a version of the origin story of the Kasihtas, translated eastward from the Chattahoochee and updated for the political realities of the 1770s. So even if it is true that Ocmulgee was somewhat to the east of the place where different groups of Mississippian-descended peoples forged a new, yet still pluralist identity, the place was clearly important to Muskogean-speakers and they claimed ancient connections to the site. It follows that among modern nations, the Muscogee (Creek) Nation maintains the strongest connection to Ocmulgee.

Whether or not Muskogee-speakers and others founded a "nation," or a "confederacy," or were more a group of autonomous towns coalescing on the Chattahoochee, then the Ocmulgee, then the Chattahoochee again, is a matter hotly debated among scholars. Eventually certain groups of Creeks would come to see Ocmulgee as the birthplace of a shared identity, and would use this interpretation to protect a place they viewed as sacred and to protect Creek lands more generally. How do we get from multiple towns of Muskogean-speakers (and others) to terms like "Creek" and "Ocmulgee"? Muskogean-speakers in the eighteenth century referred to the Ocmulgee River as *Ochese-hatchee*, and it first appears in European sources as the Ochese (sometimes Ocheesee) or Uchisi/Chachisi. When English traders first encountered the Muskogean-speakers on the river, they referred to them as the "Ocheesee Creek" Indians. While the Ocheesee part faded, the Creek part stuck, and, after the migration back to the Chattahoochee, the English would use the term "Lower Creeks" to describe the people and distinguish them from "Upper Creeks" to the north and west. Today, the Muscogee (Creek) Nation, itself a multiethnic polity like the ones from which it developed, uses "Muscogee" as a reference to its ethnic origins and the language of some of its early towns, and "Creek" as a nod to the Ocmulgee River country, which played a key role in forming a collective identity as "Creek." The name "Ocmûlgui" appears on a Spanish list of Apalachicola towns on the Chattahoochee in 1675, and as "Ocmulque" on a similar list from 1685. The Anglicized "Ocmulgee" would eventually replace these and be used to refer to the Ochese River as well.

OCMULGEE FIELD POEM

WILLIAM BARTRAM REPLIES TO A LETTER, 1791

> *. . . As to whether my Indian hosts have art,*
> *their best enwraps their bodies,*
> *for they print tattoos on their persons*

of great delicacy and effect.
The moon and planets hang upon
a great man's chest, rippling
with the movement of his muscles.
Figures also of alligators, panthers,
and forked-eye falcons invest their skins,
not rendered with the line but with the point,
the countenance of each fierce beast
being a constellation of sooty pricks—gar teeth
or quill of porcupine the pen. Ash in oil
is the only ink I know, though brighter hues
of blue, green, and red they mix in mystery.
These motes particulate into wholes—
so fearsome and elegant their effect!
They walk about like lettered scrolls,
their backs stippled with the knoll
of an epic battle. A silent man sitting fireside
flickers with stories. You wonder whether
these rinse away: they do not. The gar's needly
jaw grazes the blood with raw eternal ink.
Forever after is the man thus written.

* * * * *

The peoples who would eventually be labeled Creek drew on deep Mississippian reserves in clearly recognizable ways. As it had for their ancestors, corn took on a significant dietary, and even spiritual, role, as evidenced by Green Corn (*poskita* or busk) ceremonialism. Every year when the first corn crop was edible (the timing could vary by latitude or other factors), the ceremonial calendar reset. The people alternated between feasting and fasting, danced, forgave debts and had them forgiven, and undertook maintenance on mounds or other public structures. The town's central fire, an earthly embodiment of the sun, would be extinguished and a new one rekindled, symbolizing the renewal of the world and the people. Like their Mississippian ancestors, Creeks also partook of Black Drink, a tea (or more properly a decoction, since it's not made with tea leaves) brewed with yaupon holly. Yaupon holly is the only caffeinated plant indigenous to North America, and many

CREEK STICKBALL The stick-ball game called for great athleticism and endurance and was much more than a sporting event among Native peoples of southeastern North America, to whom it was known as "the little brother of war." Played only once a year between opposing chiefdoms of "different fires," often after weeks of negotiating the terms of the contest, the ball game mattered; a town that lost three or four times to another town became of the same fire as the winning town. Ball players endured elaborate ceremonial scratching, a ritual washing, and other preparations before a match. To take on vision, speed, quickness, and power, players wore eagle feathers, deer or cougar tails, and the rattle of a snake. The game ended when one team scored twelve points, which could take as long as eight hours. Creek artist Fred Beaver was born in Eufaula, Oklahoma, in 1911. Upon returning from service in Italy during World War II, Beaver took up painting as a hobby. In 1960, he retired from the Bureau of Indian Affairs and became a full-time artist. His works reside in collections around the world. He gave this painting to Ocmulgee in the late 1950s. (Courtesy National Park Service, Ocmulgee National Monument).

MISTIPPEE Charles Bird King's 1826 portrait of Mistippee, son of Yoholo-Micco, shows the dignity and style of male Creek clothing. Note also the tattooing on the young man's face. Muscogee men and women were often stippled with circles and other representational geometric designs along their faces, chests, arms, and legs. William Bartram describes tattoos of scrolls, snakes, suns, and battles. The very precise designs were made by pricking the skin with gar teeth or other needles dipped in red cinnabar or lamp black. Although Mistippee is pictured with a bow and arrows, he was particularly known for his mastery of hunting with the blowgun.(Courtesy University of California Library via archive.org.)

YAUPON HOLLY Mark Catesby painted Yaupon holly (*ilex vomitoria*) for his monumental *Natural History*, published from the 1720s to the 1740s). The only source of caffeine native to North America, yaupon leaves and twigs were dried, roasted in a clay pot, and steeped in hot water to brew cussena, a dark brown to black drink that was shared by leading males on ritual occasions such as the Green Corn ceremony or busk and before council meetings. The men, starting with the Miko, would drink from a large conch shell cup. When consumed in such quantity that it induced vomiting, Cussena was a means of purification. Consumed in smaller amounts, the effect is akin to that of a mild stimulant. Seminoles, in whose territory yaupon did not flourish, made their version of the drink from leaves of lizard's tail, red bay, and blueberry. (Courtesy Smithsonian Libraries via archive.org.)

Native Southeasterners recognized its stimulating effects. Europeans bestowed the scientific name *ilex vomitoria* on it, because when they witnessed its use, they saw priests and soldiers taking it in huge quantities and vomiting it up as a way of purifying themselves. Taken in small doses, the beverage has no such emetic effect. Finally, like their Mississippian ancestors, Creeks were connected to mound architecture, even if the large-scale mounds of earlier times were no longer being built. The Muskogee term for Mississippian mound, *ekvn-like* (literally "earth placed" or "earth sitting"), joins *ekvnv* (earth/world) with *liketv* (dwelling/residence/sitting), and gives heightened meaning to the sentiment that the Creeks "sat down" at Ocmulgee, or anywhere, for that matter. Mounds also feature prominently in stories of Muskogee origins.

OCMULGEE FIELD NOTE

THE FIRST FLUTE

(This story was told by Muscogee storyteller William Harjo, who plays flutes made of river cane that he crafts himself. Sometimes he finds cane that woodpeckers have already drilled a few flute-holes in. The story was told on September 7, 2016 at the Ocmulgee Indian Festival, where it was recorded and transcribed by Stephanie Ramdin.)

A long time ago there was a man, who had strong feelings for a girl and no matter what he did, she would not pay him any attention. And so, he went to an elder or maybe the medicine man in his village to tell him about his feelings. And he was told, "If you really have pain in your heart for this girl, you should go on a vision quest."

So, this is what the young man was doing. He was out in the forest for four days seeking his visions, when he heard a strange sound. And we don't know what the sound was like. It could've been like this.

[Mr. Harjo plays a few lines of music on his cane flute.]
And for all we know it could have been like this.
[Mr. Harjo plays different lines of music.]

So, whatever it was, it got his attention. By the way, that was Beethoven. And, it got his attention, so he followed it and it led him to a place where river cane was growing. Now, river cane is a plant that is originally from here. It's not a transplant from any other country. And it dates all the way back to B.C. — before Columbus. All the natives that live all over along the Gulf Coast here in the Southeast part of the United States used this for many different things -- like basket weaving by the Choctaws, blowguns by the Cherokee. So, this plant was something that was really important to us. . . .This young man saw that there was a piece of river cane and what had happened was, a tornado came through and broke some of the river cane in half. And as it was starting to dry out, some insects moved inside the decaying river cane and left some larva which grew into little animals. And the woodpecker come along and for survival put holes into the river cane to retrieve the little animals for food. And now the wind spirit was coming along passing over and through the holes to make the sounds. So the young man thought it was something special. So he took that piece of cane and he was taking it back to his village and as he was doing this, he was trying to experiment and make sounds like he had heard from the wind spirit. And as he was doing this, the young girl heard the beautiful sound and couldn't resist and came to him. So that was the beginning of the first flute. And this is a love song.

[Mr. Harjo plays a lilting love song on the cane flute.]

* * * * *

At least eleven distinct towns existed along the Ocmulgee between 1690 and 1715. A core of Muskogee and Hitchiti-speaking towns appear to have moved into the vicinity of the pre-existing Ichisi town. It bears mentioning that among Muskogee-speakers, "town" or talwa (*tvlwv*) was, and remains, a marker of identity beyond a geographical designation. They arranged themselves in much the same alignment they had on the Chattahoochee. Thus, the Muskogee-speaking towns of Coweta, Kasihta, Tuskegee and Kolomi settled north of the Ocmulgee mounds, perhaps in what's now Jones County. The southern towns, home to Hitchiti speakers, settled directly around the mounds, and on both sides of the river. These towns included Hitchiti, Ocmulgee, and Osuchi. During the two decades on the Ocmulgee, these were joined by other Muskogee-speakers: Atasi and Kealedji towns moved from the Tallapoosa River country. Refugees from other language groups settled other towns in the area. These included some Westos, the former trading and slaving partners of English Carolina, and Yuchis, who, although currently part of the Muscogee Nation, remain culturally distinct and speak a language with no clear connections to any other.

The Spanish made an attempt to punish the Ocmulgee towns in 1694, but their raid netted fifty captives before losing the element of surprise, and the people of the other towns burned their dwellings and fled into the woods before the Spanish advance. It's possible that after that date the people along the Ocmulgee were so well armed that another attack would have been too costly. The move indicated a clear refutation of the Spanish and an equally clear desire to have access to English trade goods. The people on the Chattahoochee had been participants in low volume, indirect trade with the Spanish for a long time, but this move put them squarely in line for high volume direct trade with the English. One might also read into the location a desire to get closer to English trade without getting too close to the English.

Judging from archaeological and documentary evidence, and relying on the work of scholars who study trade, it's possible to construct a list of the trade goods that the people on the Ocmulgee desired from the English, and those items that the English desired in return. The people at Ocmulgee brought deerskins and human captives and exchanged them for firearms, cloth, and metal tools. Because Carolina's plantation economy and agricultural exports such as rice and indigo eventually dominated the eighteenth century, it's sometimes easy to overlook the hundreds of thousands of deerskins and the tens of thousands of Native slaves that were the economic engines of early English Carolina.

Of course, goods do not trade themselves. They, and the trade that brings them, are enmeshed in systems of human values. European and Native American ideas about trade didn't

Gun parts (cock and mainspring) were among the fascinating items excavated at Ocmulgee's Trading Post. As soon as they made their entrance, firearms became a vital part of English trade with Native peoples in the Southeast. (Courtesy National Park Service, Ocmulgee National Monument.)

always match up, but that did not preclude members of both groups from working together to mutual advantage. We assume too much if we assume that English and Native American ideas about trade were either frozen in time or totally incompatible. To trade on the Ocmulgee, the English would have had to learn the language—probably a trade pidgin based on Muskogee—and customs of the people whose deerskins and captives they so desperately wanted. Similarly, while Native people had held captives as status symbols since Mississippian times, people were not for sale until the advent of merchant capitalism in the Southeast opened a market for human beings. The world of trade that grew up in sites like Ocmulgee was neither wholly English nor indigenous but reflected some aspects of the various groups that participated in it.

Archaeological and documentary evidence specific to Ocmulgee would seem to confirm the picture for the region as a whole. The English stationed at Ocmulgee were few and were surrounded by hundreds of people for whom Muskogee functioned as a lingua franca. To insist that business be conducted in English would be foolish. The trading post itself was likely erected according to an English design using Native labor. The goods found inside, and in the town site adjacent to the trading house, represent a rich mix of items of English, Spanish, and indigenous manufacture. English artifacts include pipe stems, bowls, knives, and gun parts. Spanish ceramics and tools were also found at the site. Items of indigenous manufacture include Ocmulgee Fields pottery.

When it comes to the traders themselves, our knowledge is hampered by the dearth of documentation. We know one name with certainty: James Lucas. He appears sporadically in the colonial records. In 1710, he complained before the Commissioners of the Indian Trade that John Musgrove "detain[ed] two Slaves unjustly from him" in a letter written from "Oakmalgoes." In 1713, he sold slaves to John Wright, and in early 1717 he was trading in Cherokee country. Lucas's possible business associates John Pight and Anthony Probat (or Probert) have left behind an even scantier documentary record. Together, the three were charged by the Commons House of Assembly with illegally enslaving twenty Indians in 1706. The charges stemmed from an incident in which Probat, Musgrove, and Pight bought as slaves a group of ostensibly free people. The governor ordered the captives released, and the traders refused: "Yet they or Some or one of them Contemptuosly and willfully disobey'd the afforesaid Commands to the great danger and Hazard of this Collony, by provokeing the Indians in Such a manner and made Some Slaves after they or one of them were made acquainted with said Order." Probat, Musgrove, and Pight were at least indicted, while James Lucas was not, and none of the indictees appear to have actually been prosecuted. To obfuscate matters further, if an Ocmulgee account book exists for the early eighteenth century, it has yet to be discovered.

The Commons House was rightfully worried that unscrupulous trade could provoke violence, as it had done before the first decade of the eighteenth century, and would do again in the conflagration of the Yamasee War, which erupted in 1715. In the second decade after the establishment of the Ocmulgee trading post, though, Muskogees and English acted in concert against a common enemy. From the perspective of the Spanish, and their allied mission Indians, the most spectacular export coming out of the towns along the Ocmulgee was violence. When the English entered into the Southeast in the 1670s, they came into a world that had been remade by violence several times over. While indigenous polities had gone to war, the level of death associated with European violence combined with the imperatives of the slave market to bring about a particularly toxic environment in the Southeast. English-allied Native people traveled long distances to commit violence and carry off captives. From the English perspective, these raids served a couple of useful purposes: they furthered

MOORE'S RAID One of the chief exports of the English colony at Charles Town was violence. Native communities were both victims and perpetrators depending on the circumstances. During Queen Anne's War, Carolina Governor James Moore in 1704 led a Creek force against several Spanish missions in what is now Florida, overwhelming the catholicized Apalachees and a small force of Spanish cavalry and essentially ending the Spanish threat to English Carolina. This is one of several vibrant dioramas which Ned Jenkins created for Ocmulgee in the years after World War II. (Courtesy National Park Service, Ocmulgee National Monument.)

imperial aims in the Southeast and they turned a profit. And in 1702 and again in 1704, the Ocmulgee trading post was at the center of it all.

The backstory of the 1702 conflict is complex. On an imperial level, the Southeast was a front in the war between England and Spain that English colonists would call Queen Anne's War. Locally, it involved Spanish restrictions on trade. Spanish-allied Apalachees were allowed to trade with English-connected Apalachicolas, but only certain items that the Spanish thought the English would have no interest in. Apalachicolas responded to the restriction by killing

Apalachee diplomats, and in spring 1702, Apalachicolas launched an attack on the mission village of Santa Fe, in Timucua province, burning most of the town and the church. A letter from Joseph de Zúñiga y Zerda, the governor of Florida, to the king describes a scene of devastation: the English and their allies made "an attack on the convent with many firearms and arrows and burning the church, although not the images which with some risk were saved." The first attempt at retaliation was a failure, but the second, in October 1702, was a catastrophe that prefigured the collapse of the entire mission province. In this particular assault, a force of about 800 Apalachees set out to punish the Apalachicolas, but they were routed by a smaller, better-armed force led by an unnamed Englishman. This battle occurred near the near the confluence of the Flint and Chattahoochee. One source puts the number of Apalachees captured and killed at 600. Many of the survivors fled haphazardly toward the mission towns, leaving their weapons behind. There is good reason to believe that the force originated at Ocmulgee, and that the captives passed through that town on their way to Charles Town.

The details of the 1704 battle are better documented, and they are gory. The proceedings near the town of Ayubale in January 1704 were particularly so. Soldiers from Ocmulgee burned sixteen prisoners, and cut out their eyes, tongues, and ears. This kind of violence was not undertaken lightly, and Muskogee torture had deep, even Mississippian roots. The method chosen for these captives' execution obviously inflamed Spanish passions, and could be used to further the Spanish argument that Native Americans were in need of continued religious instruction to tame their allegedly savage nature. The event was probably not so simple from a Muskogee perspective. The practice of torture was widespread in the Southeast, and both early modern Native Americans and Europeans took trophies from their defeated enemies. Torture fulfilled a different role in Native American communities, though. Torture, far from being a dehumanizing act, could be the exact opposite. The fact that such great care was taken in dispatching victims might even be seen as a way of recognizing a common humanity. Among later Creeks, torture served a crucial function: it allowed aggrieved parties to grieve publically the wrongs done them, and it allowed men to prove their bravery as they left this world. For many groups, the ritual death was a way of bringing episodes of violence to a close.

English involvement in the Southeast raised the stakes of indigenous violence considerably. Thomas Nairne, who would die by torture at the outset of the Yamasee War, described the English strategy in 1705 when he noted that "We have these two . . . past years been intirely kniving all the Indian Towns in Florida which were subject to the Spaniards and have even accomplished it." Native Americans had gone to war for a very long time, but their goals in warfare rarely involved "intirely kniving" towns before the English arrived. Even during the longer campaigns, involving higher risk battles that the English preferred, Native ideas about violence were not entirely absent. From an indigenous perspective, careful, ritually performed torture might have been the proper way to take the lives of Florida mission Indians, while the English would have probably preferred that they be kept alive to be sacrificed to sugar plantations on Barbados or elsewhere.

Though Ayubale was the first town to be attacked, it was not the only one. In June and July, James Moore and the Ocmulgee army returned and Tomole, Capoli, Tama, and Ocatosis suffered, and lost as many as 1,000 people. For his part, Moore claimed 4,000, but 3,000 seem to have disappeared between the missions and Charles Town. The exact number of captives carried off in Moore's 1704 campaigns is probably irrecoverable at this remove, but it was clearly in the hundreds, while some sources suggest it rose into the thousands. Some Apalachees simply chose not to fight the English, having grown disillusioned with Spanish governance. One group went so far as to say that if the English ever came, they would burn the Spanish in their fort and escape: "if they remain until the return of the enemy, it will be in order [to go] against us, and they will burn us within the blockhouse, while they escape with their lives." Approximately 1300 Apalachees, 300-plus men and 1000 women and children, joined the retreating army as it passed through Ocmulgee on the way to Charles Town. The result was that the missions were depopulated, the Spanish hold on the interior Southeast grew tenuous, and the English-Muskogee alliance strengthened, albeit temporarily. At a treaty signed at Coweta, leaders of most of the Ocmulgee towns formally pledged to assist the English.

The trading post and the towns around it begin to fade from our view in the 1710s. As quickly as the site was built up in the 1690s, it was abandoned in the 1710s in the era of the Yamasee War. The conflict began with the widespread, coordinated killings of English traders by Yamasees and others, including, almost certainly, the traders working at Ocmulgee. The Yamasees and their allies eventually killed hundreds of English (and even approached Charles Town), but the Native coalition weakened when Cherokees chose to ally themselves with the English to war against the Creeks, and the Yamasees were eventually forced to disperse. The towns that had aggregated at Ocmulgee moved back to the Chattahoochee country. While the period between 1690 and 1715 witnessed spasms of violence and ended with Ocmulgee once again depopulated, it's possible to argue that it prepared subsequent generations of Muskogees to resist English colonialism in some sophisticated ways. Ocmulgee continued to hold sway over Muskogee minds as a crucial place in forming a shared identity. There were long-standing linguistic, cultural, and, by this point, historical ties between the various towns that came together on the Ocmulgee, including certain social structures and practices that were holdovers from the Mississippian era.

From a British perspective, the violence of the Yamasee War and the persistence of the Spanish colony in Florida demonstrated a need to solidify the empire's hold on the Atlantic coast. To that end, and to serve as a social experiment of sorts, the colony of Georgia was established in 1733. That event affected Ocmulgee's history very little in the short term, but it would have far-reaching long-term consequences. While the English trading post was squarely in Creek territory, it did not signal any claims to that territory. As the colony of Georgia expanded, it would begin to pressure Creeks for their land, including the sacred space at Ocmulgee.

PART 5

LOSING AND FINDING OCMULGEE

In the 1770s, Ocmulgee, though no longer occupied physically by Creeks, was still an important meeting place between Creeks and their white neighbors. Creek people continued to attach spiritual significance to the site as well, though not always in a positive sense. James Adair, whose 1775 *History of the American Indians*... (the original title continues for several dozen more words) is by turns illuminating and hard to decipher (he believed in an ancient connection between Hebrews and Native Americans), had the following to say about the site. After chiding Native Americans for their "superstitious" nature, Adair treats supernatural occurrences "at *Okmulge*, the old waste town, belonging to the *Muskohge*, 150 miles S. W. of Augusta in Georgia, which the South Carolinians destroyed about the year 1715." (In all likelihood, Creeks and others had seized the stores and burned the outpost before moving to the Chattahoochee.) There, "they strenuously aver, that when necessity forces them to en camp there, they always hear, at the dawn of the morning, the usual noise of Indians singing their joyful religious notes, and dancing, as if going down to the river to purify themselves, and then returning to the old town-house." Adair never heard the ghostly singing himself: "Whenever I have been there, however, all hath been silent," perhaps because he was "an obdurate infidel that way."

The thought would not be complete without adding that "the Hebrews seem to have entertained notions pretty much resembling the Indian opinions on this head."

OCMULGEE FIELD NOTE

MINUS

The old man has walked the mounds for years, breathing hard on the hills. The bugsong and the breezes encourage him through his aches. They make him feel more alive in his body. He likes the aloneness, which varies as he passes through different rooms of the landscape—the big, mowed meadow, the stretch of hardwood forest, the smooth road, the ferny stream he crosses in the woods. His solitude here brings back his boyhood, when he swam the river. His stride takes small bites of earth that build up into his daily two miles.

The spirits of the place follow him in his morning habit, minus their bodies, minus their old shapes and forms. In the old man's people's stories about death, dying is going away, becoming absent. He doesn't know that the native spirits never leave. His hard breathing and sweat draw them down from the pines, up from their graves in the clay floors of the mud-daub houses long gone now, up from the funeral mound. The dead miss the pleasure of sweating as they miss the other warm dews of the body. Sweat is an incense that wakes them, though they never sleep. They are not disquieted or vengeful. They are not ghosts. They are of the place, in it as they ought to be, because it is their only place, what they are made from, what they first came from, and where they have gone. Their only distress is the absence of the living who know of them and carry on their names and ways, who balance their posthumous-ness with running, loving, craft, feeding big families, with war. To be dead and unremembered is awful.

Many native peoples did not speak of their people once they passed. They kept courtesy by not speaking of them, because they were still nearby and would suffer from hearing their names spoken by the living. The people new to this place—the spirits had called these newcomers "white foam people" because they were blown in off the sea—don't know that they don't know, but a few, like this old man, this walker, have natures open enough to sometimes sympathize with the people who have passed. The old man feels the other world contained in this one. He feels that there is more than one kind of time.

The spirits do not harm the old man. What is harm to them anyway? They do not manifest themselves to him at all except as a pleasant coolness and a fog visible where the rays of the sun slant through it. He thinks the chill is simply the first freshness of fall. The spirits are drawn into his lungs, then breathed back out, wisps of them, a precipitation of soul that would have many faces if it had any face at all. He feels minus. Also met.

* * * * *

THE BIRTH OF THE UNITED STATES AND CREEK COUNTRY

Looking westward from Savannah, the seat of government, at around the same time James Adair's work was published, the Ocmulgee site teetered at the far southwestern edge of England's southernmost mainland colony, and was not in the immediate path of white colonization. Just a few years later, the newly independent United States and the state of Georgia were in the process of acquiring as much Native land as possible for white settlement and extinguishing Indian land claims as a way of consolidating their power. No fighting in the American War for Independence took place at Ocmulgee, but Creeks by and large sided with the British in that conflict. This was not because Creeks had any great affection for the British Empire, but they justifiably feared the territorial aspirations of the United States. Creek diplomacy in the years after the war was characterized by an attempt to maintain access to trade with Spain (and British traders operating in Florida) and the United States, often under the auspices of mixed-race leaders such as Alexander McGillivray. On the American side, during the administrations of Washington, Adams, and Jefferson, the United States exerted cultural pressure on Native Americans through its "civilization program." The program took its cues from an Enlightenment philosophy that perceived Indian behavior, not Indian-ness itself, as the main obstacle to Native peoples integrating into the United States. Once Native people gave up hunting, the theory went, they would become farmers and participants in the cash-crop agricultural market. Not coincidentally, their claims to land would shrink dramatically. Many early treaties between the United States and the Creeks show the influence of this policy. The 1790 Treaty of New York, for example, stipulated that the United States would provide the Creeks with "useful domestic animals and implements of husbandry." Fort Hawkins, built in the first decade of the nineteenth century, was one in a sequence of westward-moving sites from which this policy would be administered. Creek country fanned out to the west of Ocmulgee, but Creeks still came to the vicinity to deal with their American neighbors.

Fort Hawkins was a physical reminder of the expanding power of the United States vis-à-vis the Creeks, as well as an outpost of what Americans referred to as the Civilization policy. (Vintage postcard, collection of Matthew Jennings.)

The birth of the United States placed Muskogee people in a serious bind when it came to the people's homelands. In 1802, President Jefferson made American intentions plain when he promised to force Native Americans within the boundaries of Georgia to relinquish their territorial claims in exchange for the state of Georgia turning over its western claims to the federal government in the so-called Georgia Compact. In Article One, Section 4, the federal government staked a claim to the land between the Oconee and Ocmulgee Rivers, including the Ocmulgee mound complex; the section concluded ominously: "the United States shall, in the same manner, extinguish the Indian title to all the other lands within the State of Georgia." By 1802, Muskogees faced pressure to sell land from multiple fronts: the United States government, the state government of Georgia, and increasing numbers of white settlers and their slaves encroaching on their territory.

As early as the 1780s, white people had been dividing up Georgia's Creek lands and trespassing on Creek territory, years

Hopothle Mico was one of a number of prominent Creek leaders who negotiated the Treaty of New York with the United States in 1790. American artist John Trumbull sketched this striking image. Note the blending of Euroamerican and Native clothing, as well as the crescent-shaped gorget. (Courtesy New York Public Library.)

before any treaty gave them permission to do so. In September 1784 talks, the Tallassee King (Hoboithle Mico) expressed dissatisfaction that "the white people have been there marking the trees and running their lines, and that some of his people have been down and are much dissatisfied and blame him for

Benjamin Hawkins administered American policy, the so-called "Civilization" policy, in Creek country from several different locations in the late eighteenth and early nineteenth centuries. Though fairer-minded than many of his fellow Americans, Hawkins still harbored prejudices against his Native "charges." Even so, his writings remain a valuable source of historical information about the Creeks. (The Plan of Civilization, unknown artist, c. 1800, oil on canvas, 35.875" x 49.875", Courtesy Greenville County Museum of Art, South Carolina.)

giving away their rights." Hoboithle Mico was willing to accept some white settlement, with an important qualification: "When the Oconee land is settled he hopes it will be with good white people." In 1790, an anonymous Creek leader (perhaps Hoboithle Mico) sent a "Memo of the Kings Proposals and Complaints" to Georgia's legislature. The memorial complained that "instead of the white people being contented with that very great tract of country he and his people had agreed to give them he was sorry to find they had been marking land as far as the water of the Oakmulge river."

Individual white Georgians were invading what remained of Creek Country in Georgia. John Galphin wrote from Rock Landing, on the Oconee River, in summer 1789 that white people were continually approaching the Ocmulgee to "disturb the Indians when peaceably hunting." Galphin concluded that "it is much the best for the white people to keep on their side of the river." Predictably, small-scale violence was the result of continual white encroachment. The violence cut both ways, though the surviving written records obscure this fact and blame hostilities largely on Creeks: multiple thick volumes of "Indian Depredations" dating to the late eighteenth and early nineteenth centuries line the shelves at Georgia's Department of Archives and History. A particularly ugly incident from 1793 involved a Creek hunting party between the Ocmulgee and Oconee Rivers. The party of nine Creeks entertained white guests, "show[ing] them every attention in their power"; the guests returned the favor by leaving for a brief time, then returning with a well-armed group of white men, who killed two Creeks immediately and sent the other seven running for their lives.

Focusing solely on the violence that wracked the border regions of Creek territory runs the risk of overshadowing the fact that other developments were taking place simultaneously in Creek Country. Creek Indians and white Americans were moving, trading, and fighting in a world that was neither wholly Creek nor wholly American. Some Creeks, whatever their skin color or ethnic background, managed to live in Creek *talwas* while at the same time participating in a regional, even trans-Atlantic economy. Matrilineal clans and communal property were weakening in the face of a national or racial identity and individual property passed from father to son. The significance of the decision to finally relinquish the territorial claim to Ocmulgee might best be understood in this larger context. It seems unlikely that the decision to give up Ocmulgee in the 1820s—after keeping it in every prior treaty—was just a coincidence. The momentous decision to "leave" Ocmulgee was undertaken in a fraught historical atmosphere. Giving up Ocmulgee may have meant more than just giving up a sacred site, more than a site with historical significance. It may have meant giving up much more: the notion that white people and Native Americans could co-exist in or near the United States.

Ocmulgee played a key role in the delicate negotiations pertaining to the Treaty of Washington, the 1805 agreement that formalized the cession of most of the land between the Oconee and Ocmulgee Rivers. In a note to the Senate, Thomas Jefferson pointed out that the Creeks were not only an important tribe to maintain peaceful, friendly relations with but also one of the tribes "most fixed in the policy of holding fast their lands." It was true that for more than a decade since the Treaty of New York in 1790, the Creeks had steadfastly refused any land cessions. Even so, some parts of their land appear to have been more valuable than others. The treaty, which many in the Creek Nation would disavow, and for which one of the signers would pay with his life, reserved a "tract of land four miles in length, and two in width, bordering on the river, to include the Oakmulgee old fields." Hopoy Micco, who would eventually sign the treaty and be killed for doing so, wrote to Benjamin Hawkins that "the tract of land at Oakmulgee old fields is ours; we have reserved it to meet and trade with our white friends."

Many simmering issues boiled over in the Creek Civil War of the 1810s. In the aftermath of the toughest fighting, Creeks from both the Upper and Lower Towns lost massive amounts of territory in the Treaty of Fort Jackson, signed at bayonet point in 1814. The United States solidified its military control over the Southeast, further marginalizing Native Americans. And within the Creek Nation itself, the pace of change accelerated dramatically. Divisions between elite Creeks and commoners widened, and divisions between Upper Towns and Lower Towns grew.

Before the outrageous, illegal, and abrogated 1825 Treaty of Indian Springs, and the legal and ratified 1826 Treaty of

Washington that confirmed the sale of the remaining Creek lands in Georgia, Creek peoples had managed to hold on to the Ocmulgee site, while ceding everything around it, leaving an island of nominally Creek space in the expanding sea of Georgia. This should not be taken to mean that Muskogee people continued to inhabit the Ocmulgee site year-round—they had not lived there for decades. Rather, delegations of Creeks traveled to Ocmulgee regularly. Doing so indicated that the fields and monuments at Ocmulgee had taken on a symbolic significance. The mounds and environs symbolized the Creek Nation's connection to its Mississippian past. They also functioned as a meeting place between Creeks and agents of the United States for purposes of communication and trade.

LEAVING OCMULGEE

In their century-long occupation of the Ocmulgee site before it became protected federal land, white people did not take particularly good care of the site. To be blunt, the people near the site cared more for its value as planting land, railroad right of way, and possible use as a pleasure ground than anything it might teach them about American antiquity. There were voices of opposition: the occasional newspaper editorial or amateur archaeologist reported on a find of some significance and called for the preservation of the site. These voices were drowned out by those who favored exploitation over stewardship. We shouldn't necessarily be surprised at this, given the premium placed on progress and modernization during this time period in the United States.

In 1819, thousands of Creeks gathered at Fort Hawkins and Ocmulgee Old Fields to receive their annuity from the United States. A citizen of Milledgeville, Georgia, recalled his visit to the massive encampment more than three decades later, in 1851: "On the evening of my arrival I saw the big warrior, the most striking specimen of Indian greatness, the Little Prince, the speaker of the tribe, and its greater orator, and General McIntosh, its most Gallant chief." This anonymous citizen of Milledgeville described a remarkable scene, as "many thousand Indians were standing or squatted in little groups around fires which the coldness of the morning made necessary for comfort." At a certain point, a deer bounded through the camp, and the chronicler wrote wistfully, "they gave such a yell as will never again reverberate along the banks of the Ocmulgee river." To drive home the point, the narrative lurches ahead to the 1850s, by which point "warehouses, bank houses, churches, colleges, splendid dwelling houses, shops of business now stand where trees then stood." The *Milledgeville Recorder's* editor followed the remembrance with some ethnography of his own: "when the old man who writes was young, more than half of the territory of the State was occupied by Indians, the least improvable of all the races of men. They are all gone. The places which once knew them is [sic] now occupied by the best population of the most improved countries. If the glorious promise derived from the past shall be realized in the future, Georgia is destined to be the brightest star in the galaxy of the Union." Nine years hence, the lands would be sold in the auction that opened part 3 above.

As some white Georgians erased Native Americans from their state's recent past, Georgia and the federal government forged ahead in extinguishing all Native American land claims within the state, though the project was not complete until the forced removal of thousands of Cherokees in the late 1830s. Creeks had abandoned Ocmulgee, and had eventually been driven from the region in a brutal process of ethnic cleansing that lasted for decades (and remained incomplete—several remnant communities persist). In the years surrounding removal, the Creek Nation stared down a variety of existential threats, and while the town names, including Okmulgee, and a town-based identity would have been recognizable to the ancestral Creeks, the challenges were of a vastly different nature. Simply put, ancestral Creeks had labored to build a Creek identity (whether a confederacy or a nation remains open to interpretation) in the seventeenth and eighteenth centuries, and nineteenth-century Creeks were engaged in an existential struggle with a ferocious imperial power. We should not be surprised if mid-nineteenth-century Creeks wrote or spoke sparingly about the mounds to outsiders, even as their politics continued to be informed by the alliances that were initiated there. Some Creeks carried sorts of mound-building traditions with them, though perhaps railroad rights of way through the modern Creek Nation were of more immediate import than a mound site over 850 miles to the east.

Some early Maconites recognized that the mounds had some value, even as they puzzled over just what they represented. An 1840 editorial in the *Telegraph* opined that it really would be a shame if the mounds "were leveled by the sordid plow." Yet, despite the pleading of some white Maconites, and, one would assume, against the wishes of most Muskogee people, the land did fall under the "sordid plow." Not surprisingly, the property was divided numerous times between the initial 1828 sale and the 1930s, when the lands that would become Ocmulgee National Monument were purchased by a group consisting of the Macon Junior Chamber of Commerce, the Macon Historical Society, and a recently incorporated group called the Society for Georgia Archaeology. In the mid-1820s, a fifteen-square-mile tract on the east side of the Ocmulgee was usually denoted as "the Creek Reserve" or the "Macon Public Reserve East." At the initial sale, the poorest planting land, that which surrounded Fort Hawkins, was bundled into a hundred-acre lot and sold to Thomas Woolfolk for $2,150. More desirable land closer to the Ocmulgee (and downtown Macon) sold for between $700 and $1,000 an acre.

Among the purchasers of these lots were Roger and Eliazar McCall, two flatboat entrepreneurs. After this initial sale, for which the records are sketchy, the threads of who owned which part of the site get even harder to weave together. By the 1860s, Samuel Dunlap, an entrepreneur and planter, had accumulated major landholdings at the site. Other serious players in the area included two of the powerful Lamar clan and the aforementioned Thomas Woolfolk. According to the 1860 census, more than two hundred enslaved people worked cotton fields that stretched as close to the marshland as was practicable. Further research will be needed to determine the specific impact of plantation agriculture on the site, but decades of cotton planting clearly had detrimental effects. Repeated cotton seasons stripped away topsoil and sped erosion. Still, the most damaging intrusion occurred in two bursts of activity in 1843 and 1873, as the Central of Georgia Railroad and its subcontractors sliced through the Muskogees' sacred land in the holy name of profits.

To the architects of the Central Railroad, the mounds on the east side of Macon represented an engineering obstacle to be overcome, and there is fragmentary, though somewhat persuasive, evidence that the railroad's planners knew that the mounds were human creations. A 1930s Central of Georgia publication mentioned cavalierly that in the building of the railroad, "the construction forces cut right through one of the largest mounds, probably considering it as 'just another hill' blocking progress." It's probably more accurate to say that the engineers understood that the mound was made by people, but didn't care enough about the people who made it to avoid destroying it. As factions on the road's board debated various routes into Macon, the Central sent a surveying team through Georgia's interior. The maps show that the ground east of Macon was quite high compared to the surrounding areas, and the surveyor appears to have distinguished the mounds, which were squared off, from the hills, which were irregularly shaped, but there are few named features on the map. An 1866 diagram of the entire route of the Central (drawn up to prepare for postwar repairs, one imagines) shows deep cuts approaching Macon, gives some property owners' names, and points out Macon's main thoroughfares—Wharf (today's Riverside Drive), Walnut, and Mulberry Streets—but is silent regarding the mounds and ancient fields. There is also a fleeting reference to a "great Mound" in the November 1840 annual report. The word "mound," as understood by white Americans in the nineteenth century, often referred to ancient earthworks.

The Muskogees' songs might not have reverberated along the banks of the Ocmulgee in the mid-nineteenth century, but visitors to the land east of Macon could have heard other music: the work songs of enslaved men as they cleared land, moved massive amounts of earth to grade the roadbed, and eventually laid the rails and drove the spikes that would bring the Central of Georgia Railroad from Savannah to Macon. In the earlier stages of construction, European immigrants and enslaved African Americans had labored alongside one another, but as the railroad moved through cotton country, the labor force became almost exclusively enslaved. The Annual Report of the Central Railroad and Banking Company for 1839 noted that to ease "sectional differences among the laborers," some contractors had "resort[ed] to the employment of blacks altogether." The board of the Central believed that African American slaves were suited to the work: "that negro labor is perfectly adapted to the construction of works of internal improvement, is now a well established fact." The use of slave labor also kept costs down, as a crew of five men and a woman could be rented, fed, and clothed for just over $60 per month. Of course, the people doing the work saw none of this meager sum, which was paid to those who owned them.

As summer 1843 turned to fall, the Central of Georgia inched toward the Ocmulgee's eastern bank (it would not cross the river until 1851). It was touted by its promoters as the longest in the world built and owned by a single company, and it appeared to herald Macon's ascent into the first rank of modern Southern towns. Just days after the first locomotive and cars arrived from Savannah at the end of a twelve-hour climb from the coast, local dignitaries gathered to mark the occasion. The mayor of Macon, John J. Gresham, spoke and ruminated "on the great conquest over time and space which was now achieved and secured forever in favor of Savannah, in her social intercourse, not only with Macon, but with a vast and fertile country, extending above and around us in every direction." Maconites clearly believed that the rails carried progress to their town and ensured its prosperous development in the future.

Progress and development had a cost. The 1843 cut runs between the largest mounds and the Earth Lodge or council house. When initially made, it destroyed an unknown amount of the Lesser Temple Mound (one 1930s estimate ranged as high as 75 percent). Because of the way the mounds were constructed, and the fact that the sloped sides support much

Today's park road runs in the 1840s railcut. This image gives viewers some idea of the depth of the cut and damage to the plateau and Lesser Temple Mound on the left. (Photograph by Matthew Jennings.)

of the structures' massive weight, the initial cut continued to do damage for decades, speeding the erosion process and leading to severe slumping of the remaining portion of the earthwork. As the railroad crews dug through the mound and the surrounding plateau, they uncovered a number of what newspaper accounts described as "ancient relics." Even given the state of archaeological understanding at the time, the treatment of the Ocmulgee site is distressing: "a large earthen pot was discovered, which would probably hold about eight gallons—but it was unfortunately broken in the excavation." Other finds included human remains: "Not far from the spot... was found a large human skeleton, but nothing near it except a large flat stone that was placed on its Head. Other human bones have also been found thereabouts in making the excavations."

The finds appear to span several of the eras of human occupation at the Ocmulgee site, but most concentrated in the Mississippian years (950–1100) and the years of the subsequent English trading post. Spoons and other items of European manufacture were turned up in the 1843 railroad dig as well. The initial damage was done, and most white Maconites looked ahead to a future based on businesses surrounding cotton agriculture and reliable trade with the coast. The Central of Georgia was a smashing success, and Macon grew as a result, even if artifacts such as eight-gallon pots had to be smashed along the way.

THE CIVIL WAR ERA, A NEW RAILROAD CUT, AND SOME EARLY ARCHAEOLOGY

The Civil War touched Macon comparatively lightly, but Union and Confederate soldiers did erect earthworks near the Ocmulgee mounds and fields, and two minor engagements were fought near the site. Samuel Dunlap had a fine residence in town, but also maintained a smaller house on his lands on the Ocmulgee's east side. As mentioned above, the primary activity in the region was cotton planting, and enslaved men and women cleared the Ocmulgee land as close to the river as was practical. The war that would bring them freedom passed their cabin doors in July 1864. General George Stoneman used the Dunlap residence as his headquarters, and Union soldiers threw up small earthworks to repel a Confederate attack. After the battle, Confederates sought to protect a nearby railroad with earthworks of their own. These were low-rising U-shaped affairs, put up in the vicinity of Samuel Dunlap's home. In November 1864, to divert attention from Sherman's march from Atlanta to Savannah, federal soldiers again visited the site. Though their presence was brief, it signaled the beginning of the end for the plantation regime at Ocmulgee and resulted in serious damage to the rail line leading into Macon. At various points in the years since, iron rails have turned up

DUNLAP HOUSE Two Civil War engagements were fought on Samuel Dunlap's East Macon property. Dunlap arrived in Macon in 1849, and made a fortune in the hardware business after the Civil War. (Courtesy National Park Service, Ocmulgee National Monument.)

CIVIL WAR SWORD One of the most appealing things about Ocmulgee is how many different eras of human history are represented by the site. This sword dates the to the Civil War. (Courtesy National Park Service, Ocmulgee National Monument.)

near the 1843 railroad bed, bearing the telltale signs of having been heated and twisted.

In the 1870s, as white Maconites attempted to rebuild their economy and African Americans probed the limits of their newly won freedom, the Central of Georgia was busy. Rather than repairing the damaged road, the Central of Georgia (technically, one of its subsidiaries, the Macon, Dublin, and Savannah Railroad) decided to move its line a couple of hundred yards to the north. The 1873 cut lies directly between what archaeologists labeled Mound D-1 (today's Earth Lodge) and the Creek Trading Post. While the 1843 cut damaged the southern end of Mound C, today's Funeral Mound, the 1873 cut seems to have totally removed its northern half. As with previous railroad activity, the 1873 cut led to further slumping of earthworks and increased erosion rates.

At least in the 1870s, historian and amateur archaeologist (both history and archaeology were academic pursuits as well as genteel hobbies as the time) Charles Colock Jones Jr. was on the scene to make drawings and record artifacts. Jones was born in 1831, the son of Mary Jones and Charles Colcock Jones. Jones the elder was a prominent Presbyterian minister and planter. During the Civil War, Jones Jr. had coordinated

At two points in Ocmulgee's history, railroad construction did irreparable damage to the ancient earthworks. This photograph captures the trauma caused by the 1870s cut. (Courtesy Vanishing Georgia, Georgia Archives)

artillery in the defense of Georgia and lost the great wealth he had in rice and cotton plantations. Following a stint practicing law in New York City, Jones settled in a small town near Augusta and produced a remarkable string of books and speeches. By the time of his death in the 1890s, he was widely regarded as Georgia's leading historian, a sought-after public speaker, and partisan of the Lost Cause. His writings about Native Americans, while more scholarly and intelligent than the speculative and bumptious newspaper coverage, do put forward Native peoples as the original Lost Causes of the South, whose demise, while unfortunate, was simply another case of a proud, well-formed people defeated not only by invasion or arms but by modernity itself. Jones's prose often approached romanticism and reverie when treating Native American history. A typical passage reads, "in obedience to the law of progress, the weaker and the more ignorant race disappears before the conquering march of the stronger and more enlightened." Jones also developed a penchant for

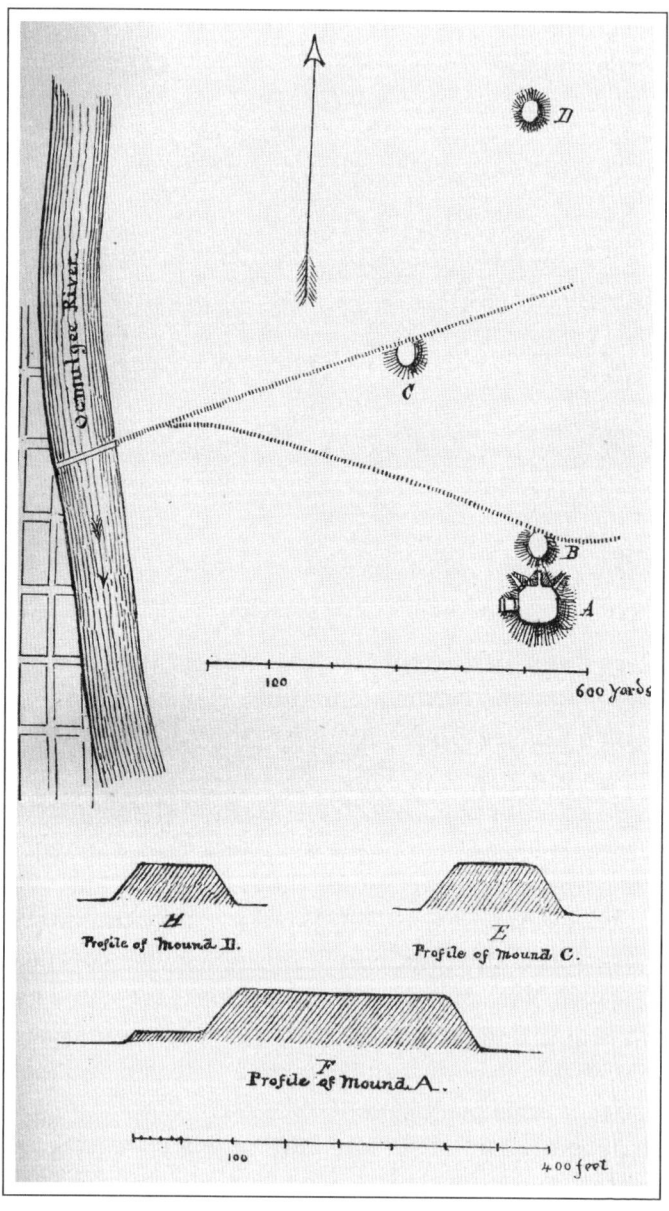

Charles Colcock Jones Jr. visited Ocmulgee around the time of the 1870s railcut, and included this drawing in his *Antiquities of the Southern Indians, Particularly of the Georgia Tribes*.(Collection of Matthew Jennings.)

putting words in the mouths of Indian characters he created: "They [white people] waste us, ay- like April snow in the warm noon, we shrink away."

Jones devoted a chapter of his *Antiquities of the Southern Indians* to the Ocmulgee site. After outlining the basics of the site and the mounds, Jones notes,

> Here, in excavating for the new track of the Central Railway, the workmen a short time since unearthed, a few feet below the surface, several skeletons, in connection with which were found beads of shell and porcelain, a part of a discoidal stone, several arrow and spear points, two stone celts, a clay pipe, an earthen pot, and other matters of a primitive character fashioned for use or ornament.

This find references at least two different eras of indigenous life. The discoidal stone may be a chunkey stone from the time the mounds were built or perhaps a later Mississippian tradition. The presence of porcelain indicates that some of the burials were associated with the Creek town at Ocmulgee. Though Jones obviously could not benefit from the decades of scholarly investigation at Ocmulgee that occurred after his death, recent investigations do bear out some of his speculations. In spite of the romanticism in which Jones's work is couched, the scholarship is solid for its time. The plates that accompanied *Southern Antiquities* hint at the damage caused by the railroad, too.

FINDING OCMULGEE

Between the 1873 railroad cut and the rekindling of interest in the site, very little is known about what went on there. The information that is available indicates that the Ocmulgee mounds and fields were incorporated into the eco-

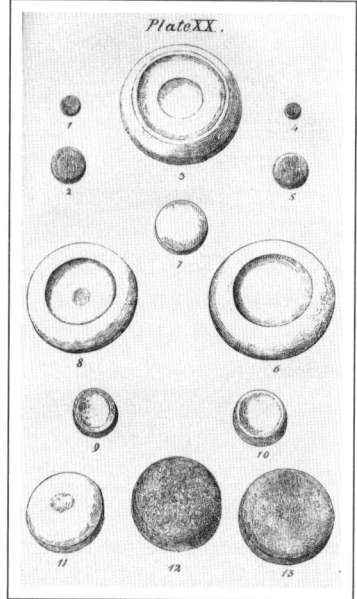 

Jones made skillful drawings of the objects unearthed during the construction of the railroad. (Collection of Matthew Jennings.)

nomic life of the region. In addition to the remnants of the farms that spread over the land prior to the Civil War (the Dunlaps retained their property though they concentrated more heavily on dairy farming than they had in the years prior to the war), and the buildings associated with the Central of Georgia, new enterprises appeared. These included an open-pit clay mine, a fertilizer factory, and, eventually, some outbuildings for the massive Bibb Mill No. 1. Economic development on the river's east side necessitated better roads, and tons of earth were removed from MacDougal Mound to use for fill dirt on Main Street. Another insult came in the early twentieth century, as young motorcyclists raced their machines up and down the Great Temple Mound, cutting deep grooves that further sped erosion. The period between the Creeks' forced abandonment of the Ocmulgee site and the sale of the site to the federal government is a dark chapter in Ocmulgee's history. Thankfully, it is not the final chapter. In the years that followed, federal archaeologists, Civil Works Administration (CWA) workers, and, most important, the Creeks themselves would lay claim to the sacred monuments and ancient fields on the east side of the Ocmulgee.

OCMULGEE FIELD NOTE

DRAKE'S FIELD

Early August 2013

Sequestration has let the grass grow at Ocmulgee—or at least kept it from being cut in all the usual places. Today when I come to the end of the bridge over the railroad cut, I find the meadow due west of the earth lodge grown six feet high with grass and brush. The sightline that usually includes the low swell of the lodge and a good part of the path beyond leading to the visitor center has been eaten up by luxurious green. The sidewalk I stand on—an open, public (though never crowded) thoroughfare for all the twenty years I have been coming to the park—has turned private. I pause between the wild canopy of muscadine vine that drips from the trees along the right side of the path and the strip of dewy, high grass on my left, all of it shaded from the mid-morning sun. Legislative and bureaucratic sequestration has freed up a field for personal and contemplative sequestration.

The Romantic poets and novelists used a word you almost never hear anymore: "bower." A room that isn't *inside, but out. This corner of the meadow feels walled and sheltered, a pleasantly confined place apart, where privacy is possible, where the apartness isn't apartness from but apartness in—apartness in a green, moist, teeming corner where growth is a rank visual clamor and a raucous competition. Everything grabs for the light. Every branch, tendril, and blade strains against its neighbor for its place, for an extra swallow of sunshine. Chlorophyll thrums, as invisible and potent as testosterone. It's as if a battle has been lost and the barbarians have trampled the gate and are burning down the town commons with green fire—except that with the collapse of one order another arises. Imagine the field mice, the insects, birds, and raccoons who are resettling this thicket, each finding food and shelter. For them, for the snakes and the fennel, sequestration is over.*

* * * * *

The situation began to change slowly in 1922, when Walter Harris, a local attorney and general in the Georgia National Guard until he retired in 1919, wrote to the Bureau of American Ethnology at the Smithsonian asking for professional archaeologists to travel to Macon to investigate the site. No immediate action followed, but in 1929, when construction crews and local schoolchildren, including some Boy Scouts, unearthed bones and beads at the site, Harris wrote again. The very next day, Scout officials also wrote to the Smithsonian, requesting expert assistance in excavating the mounds.

M. W. Stirling, then head of the Bureau of American Ethnology, traveled to Macon in April 1929 and agreed that the mounds and fields merited excavation and close study, but a lengthy, confusing, and sometimes contentious process would play out before Ocmulgee National Monument came into being. On the legislative front, in February 1934,

Representative Carl Vinson introduced legislation in committee that would have appropriated federal funds to create "Ocmulgee National Park." Secretary of the Interior Harold Ickes balked at both the name and the appropriation, suggesting "Ocmulgee National Monument" and that the land be acquired locally and then granted to the National Park Service to manage. The altered legislation passed the House without debate in May, and the Senate followed suit in June. Later that month, Franklin Roosevelt lent his approval to the measure, pending the acquisition of land.

Several local entities, including the recently formed Society for Georgia Archaeology, the Macon Historical Society, and the Junior Chamber of Commerce were already working to raise funds and pressure businesses, most notably Bibb Manufacturing (owners of the Funeral Mound) to part with their lands. Irregularities in title chains, confusion about the site boundaries, and lawsuits complicated the matter immensely, but Harris, Linton Solomon, and C. C. Harrold, among others, eventually succeeded in acquiring 678 acres. On December 23, 1936, Roosevelt proclaimed the creation of Ocmulgee National Monument. In doing so, the president quoted from the House bill, noting the "'Old Ocmulgee Fields', upon which certain Indian mounds of great historical importance are located."

Archaeological work had commenced on some parts of the site years earlier (winter 1933–1934), with Arthur Kelly (a thirty-three-year-old professional archaeologist described by one subordinate as "not...too much perverted by his Harvard training") and a student, James Ford, at the helm and the labor provided by hundreds of Civil Works Administration (a forerunner of the better-known Works Progress Administration) and later Federal Emergency Relief Administration workers. CWA workers cleared trees from Mound A and worked on the road leading to it, as well as commencing work on Mounds C and D, in December 1933. In January 1934, Kelly supervised

In 1937, prominent citizens gathered to celebrate breaking ground on the reconstructed Earth Lodge. Linton Solomon (second from left), C. C. Harrold (third from left), and Walter Harris (holding stone celt) were the men most responsible for the acquisition of the land that became Ocmulgee National Monument. (Courtesy National Park Service, Ocmulgee National Monument.)

work at the Macon Plateau while Ford, a twenty-two-year-old undergraduate student, supervised excavations at Lamar. By 1935 and into 1936, 700 workers were carrying out archaeological excavations throughout the area, including on the Macon Plateau (especially at the Trading Post), Central City Park, and Brown's Mount.

In 1937, the construction of a Civilian Conservation Corps (CCC) camp began at the site. Work at Ocmulgee was mainly for white men, though white women did contribute by identifying artifacts at Macon's City Auditorium. African American men worked on segregated construction projects, and African American women were lauded for their careful handling of

Arthur Kelly is standing on top of the council house (prior to its excavation). He would eventually serve as chief archaeologist for the National Park Service and, later, teach for decades at the University of Georgia. (Courtesy National Park Service, Ocmulgee National Monument.

artifacts at the Lamar site. Though none of the labor paid especially well, the men and women who carried it out likely appreciated whatever income it provided in the depths of the Great Depression. Life in the CCC camp was particularly regimented. Young men enrolled for six months at a time and earned $30 a month, $25 of which went to their families. They awoke to a bugle call at 6:00 a.m. for group exercise and stayed busy until the late afternoon. Some attended archaeology classes at their end of their rigorous day.

In one of the most important digs, carried out through early spring and summer 1934, workers excavated what Arthur Kelly immediately termed a "council house," a round structure with a central fire pit, a raised clay platform in the shape of a

WOMEN WORKING AT LAMAR Researchers praised the work of African American women like these pictured working at Lamar. African Americans made important contributions to archaeology and cataloging. (Courtesy National Park Service, Ocmulgee National Monument.)

EARTH LODGE EXCAVATION Excavation of the council house, or Earth Lodge, began in 1934. Here, workers are just on the edge of uncovering the magnificent bird effigy on the floor. (Courtesy National Park Service, Ocmulgee National Monument.)

bird of prey, and four huge postholes where massive white oak timbers supported the roof, which was constructed of pine and cane. Then things began to get a little weird. Eventually, nineteen such council houses were unearthed in Macon and environs, seven of which were on the land that would become Ocmulgee National Monument. Kelly, who by this time had been joined by Charles Fairbanks, was conversant with earth lodge forms from the Plains, including those built by Pawnees, Mandans and Hidatsas, but they had also read fairly deeply in historical accounts of the Southeast, many of which made reference to round council houses. In the mid-1930s, the Civilian Conservation Corps was busy at On-a-Slant at Fort Abraham Lincoln State Park in North Dakota, reconstructing earth lodges there. It is not too surprising that Kelly determined that "the structural affinity of the Macon Earth Lodge

EARTH LODGE DOME While one could dispute the historical accuracy of the Earth Lodge's reconstructed exterior, the choice to cover the floor with a concrete dome undoubtedly helped protect the floor for generations to come. (Courtesy National Park Service, Ocmulgee National Monument.)

is closer to Earth Lodges [sic] of the western United States than to the type of council and ceremonial houses described by early ethnographers for Indian tribes resident in the southeastern section of the country."

That statement may have been more or less accurate, given the relatively paltry body of evidence available. In one of the many ironies that characterize early Ocmulgee history, the reconstructed Earth Lodge at Macon became something of a model for other reconstructions in the West. Almost as soon as the floor was excavated, it began to decay, and archaeologists worked to prevent that through a variety of chemical applications, including a solution of Alvar in acetone. Archaeologists had also devised a longer-term solution in the form of a poured concrete dome that would protect the floor. Subsequent decades of archaeological work have run counter to the 1930s-era assessment of the building's architecture. It is far more likely that the original council house had earth-embanked sides and a cane roof. Piling turf on top of a council house whose roof wasn't terribly steep to begin with would present serious drainage and moisture problems in a climate like that of the Macon Plateau. Still, the concrete dome had the unquestionably significant benefit of keeping the floor reasonably well protected from the elements. Once the archaeological consensus shifted and placed the Ocmulgee Earth Lodge more definitively in the orbit of other ancient and colonial-era round council houses, why not change it? While interpretive materials, plaques and wall panels

By the early 1940s, Ocmulgee had become one of Macon's signature historical attractions. The Works Progress Administration's guide to the site reflected that fact. (Collection of Matthew Jennings.)

Over the years, the National Park Service has experimented with various ways of balancing its missions of preserving and displaying its artifacts. In this late 1960s photograph, Ranger Jim Branan leads a group of schoolchildren out on a platform above the Earth Lodge floor. Jim continues to greet visitors to Ocmulgee and share his knowledge of the site's history. (Courtesy National Park Service, Ocmulgee National Monument.)

should be updated, and some have been, Ocmulgee's Earth Lodge pays tribute both to ancient Native governments and to the changing world of archaeological scholarship. Ocmulgee National Monument is a site of sacred significance to various indigenous communities, but it is also significant to the history of the discipline of archaeology itself. One major improvement came with the radiocarbon dating of some of the original council house construction materials. Archaeologists originally estimated the council house to be approximately 500 years old, but, following the tests, this estimate had to be revised significantly, pushing the Earth Lodge date back to 1015. Even though more recent tests, presumably more accurate, have moved this date slightly closer to the present (see part 3, "Making Monuments" above), early testing made it clear that the structure was really quite old, and an artifact of the Mississippian era.

DISPLAYING OCMULGEE: MUSEUM SPACES BEFORE THE 1950S

Archaeologists working at Ocmulgee envisioned the site as an educational project from its very beginning, and Macon's boosters were continually casting about for something that would put their town on the map. In 1933, Walter Harris had gone to the Junior Chamber of Commerce and given an enthusiastic pitch (which, incidentally, also attempted to rouse Maconites from their torpor regarding the region's illustrious past). "How would this development help Macon?" Harris asked, and then answered himself, "In this way: if these historic mounts are cleared and developed, scientific societies and institutions all over the world would become interested. . . . The news would rapidly spread all over the world and people would flock here to see the most perfect relics of aboriginal culture." In the same speech, Harris also dreamed up a plan to invite modern Creek representatives to the mounds for a "great festival." From the very beginnings of Ocmulgee National Monument, science and tourism were linked inextricably. The archaeologists working at Ocmulgee also began to assemble the artifacts for possible display. In doing so, they connected the various periods of the site's history in ways that are not too different from current understandings.

The first museum at Ocmulgee was a rather thrown-together affair, essentially a work shed where curious locals could have a look at the treasures that workers pulled from the earth. After the official establishment of Ocmulgee National Monument, the federal government appropriated funds for a

WORK SHED MUSEUM Even before there was a museum at Ocmulgee, the site drew thousands of tourist. In addition to the monumental architecture, visitors could view artifacts in temporary museum set up in a work shed. (Courtesy National Park Service, Ocmulgee National Monument.)

more permanent home for the artifacts, and the shell of the current museum went up. Wartime labor and budget concerns ensured that the building would remain half-complete, lacking heat, air conditioning, or much in the way of ventilation, from 1938 to the late 1940s. To say the exhibits were spartan would be an understatement. By the end of the 1940s, however, the preparation of the site kicked into high gear, and the basic modes of representing Ocmulgee's history were coming into focus.

For most of the time since Creeks had been forced to abandon Ocmulgee, non-native people in Middle Georgia had a mainly destructive relationship with the Ocmulgee mounds and fields. The digs of the 1930s complicate that picture to an extent. While the methods employed by early archaeologists were somewhat primitive, and their treat-

The unfinished museum hosted basic displays of Ocmulgee's artifacts prior to its official opening in 1951. (Courtesy National Park Service, Ocmulgee National Monument.)

ment of human remains was far from respectful, they were scientists, not looters, and their efforts added immensely to our understanding of Ocmulgee. The end of the 1930s saw "real Indians" visit Ocmulgee. Frank Canoe, Blue Cloud, and Lone Wolf, of Sioux and Iroquois extraction, were in town to perform in a Shriners' circus. The newspaper, trafficking in stereotype, described the men as "members of a once mighty race" who "strode majestically over the rolling terrain at the monument . . . the feathers in their headdress [sic] trailing colorfully behind." At one point in the visit, the group moved inside the reconstructed council house, where "Everything became mighty real."

In the 1940s, the executive vice president of the Macon Chamber of Commerce was seeking a group of Native people who would live at the mounds as a tourist attraction. He wrote to the Department of the Interior, requesting that "a group of Indians [probably Cherokees] be brought here temporarily to live at Ocmulgee National Monument." Officials responded that "Indians could be moved from their reservation in North Carolina only upon their consent," and nothing appears to have come of the petition. Things got slightly more real in the 1950s, when larger numbers of Native Americans, most of them Creeks, began to visit the mounds. The occasion was the opening of the new museum building, billed as the "largest and most modern National Park Museum east of the Mississippi River."

OCMULGEE FIELD NOTE

SQUIRREL

The squirrel's small size and nearness to the path didn't startle me nearly as much as its stance: it faced me directly, front legs spread and on the brink of springing toward me. A steady, buzzing purr rose from its ribs and back. The instant I stopped walking and stooped toward it, it leapt to a small white oak trunk—not to escape but to see me better, for it scrabbled up to eye-level and leaned forward off the bark, its face not quite a foot from my own. I did what a person does this close to another pair of eyes. I said "hello"—or "hey," rather. I'm Southern and country.

The buzz ceased. He chuffed. I raised a bent finger toward him. He unwound down the oak and in a single arcing hop landed just below my right knee, where he clung without seeming to try to at all. I found myself eye-to-eye with him again, this time from the height of my own verticality. His toes were visible, long-clawed against my khaki nylon, as was the white patch of his chest and the chestnut fur around his mouth and down his cheeks. More than seeing him, I felt him—not a weight but a lack of weight. It was more than an encounter. I felt called on—"inhabited." Colonized. My leg was no longer my own. He would bite me if I reached down, not from fear (he was no more afraid than I was) but from the wonder and tension of the moment. It was as if an invisible violin string stretched between us. It had been plucked once. It would break if touched again. The bite would be that breaking.

His gray teeth—the line between them perfectly straight and plumb—triangulated with his large, dark, liquid eyes that were thoroughly filled by my face. His nose rippled actively, in bursts that traveled along his hide until they unscrolled out his thinly furred tail. He was a signal flag of himself. The mottle of his coloring impressed me. He had dressed better for this summit meeting than had I.

In the same microsecond I thought of gently taking hold of him, he leapt off my lower thigh, bounced from ground to tree trunk, and spiraled up the bark, all in a single fluid motion that didn't stop until he was a head higher than me. He chuffed again. I chuffed back. He looked me in the eye as he had before. I chuffed two more times, drawing him halfway down to lean off the trunk—I saw the black hooks of his rear claws that let him hang head-down—and peer at my belt buckle. Then he swirled up the oak. Whatever former life we had shared ended in that flourish, though in writing this I feel him again against my pocket.

PART 6

KEEPING OCMULGEE

Acee Blue Eagle defied easy categorization, and he wouldn't have had it any other way. He traced his descent through a long line of Creeks back to William McIntosh, but would occasionally identify as part Pawnee, perhaps to explain his appearance in Plains regalia on the public speaking circuit and as the host of a children's television program in Oklahoma. As an artist and professor, he adapted traditional Native American art styles in painting, sculpture, and ceramics to new uses, some of them brazenly commercial, such as a set of "Famous Oklahoma Indian" drinking glasses advertising Knox Oil. He could trade in, even delight in, stereotypical portrayals of Native Americans, but he could also act as a cultural ambassador, offering thoughtful critiques of the way that non-Native people thought Indians should act. And in 1951, he found himself addressing a crowd of 6,000 in Macon's City Auditorium to commemorate the opening of the museum at Ocmulgee. He started the act by raising his right hand and solemnly intoning the iconic Hollywood Indian greeting: "How." Thousands of giddy schoolchildren shrieked back: "How!" Blue Eagle then went into a routine involving failed attempts to woo a lover—his flute was broken—and various other shenanigans.

In the aftermath of his visit to Georgia, he took a more measured tone, explaining, "It was truly marvelous to visit the land of my ancestors, to see the ceremonial mound and sacred

ACEE BLUE EAGLE—acclaimed Pawnee-Creek artist, professor, and cultural ambassador—visited Ocmulgee National Monument on multiple occasions in the early 1950s. Here, he appears on the cover of the 1952 festival program. (Courtesy National Park Service, Ocmulgee National Monument.)

chamber. It filled my heart and soul with reverence. I did receive a sacred feeling to deep meaning for my people." He also encouraged Maconites to continue their efforts to reach out to Creeks in Oklahoma through events like the Indian Celebration that had just taken place. "The celebration was a more wonderful thing than the people of Macon realize," Blue Eagle wrote, "because in a short time this talk will get around to all the Creek tribe and will dispell [sic] the feeling that a few of the Creeks still hold of hate and resentment." In just a few words, Blue Eagle tapped into some of the central themes of Ocmulgee's modern history. Since its inception as a National Monument, Ocmulgee has been an important tourist attraction. Since the digs of the 1930s, it has also been a site of great significance to the field of archaeology. Even as Ocmulgee's concrete husk of a museum remained unfinished, it housed over a million artifacts. But, perhaps less well known to most visitors, the site maintains a connection to a vital Indian nation, which, thanks to the ethnic cleansing of the Southeast, most of which now resides in Oklahoma, hundreds of miles west of its ancestral heart. At various points in the second half of the twentieth century, delegations of Creeks sought to impress that fact on the site's stewards.

THE MUSEUM OPENS AND OKLAHOMA CREEKS VISIT

The unfinished museum deteriorated in the 1940s, and new construction and rehabilitation started in 1950, though not with the sense of urgency that the beleaguered superintendent Millard T. Guy might have preferred. His reports and missives of 1950 and 1951 show his desperation and wit. The Museum Branch of the National Park Service, based in Washington, DC, took control of many of the finest Ocmulgee-specific artifacts to prepare them for display when the museum opened at some future unspecified date. In his October 1950 report, Guy wrote that until the artifacts were returned, "we will take great pride in showing the public a beautiful, empty building." As late as August 1951, Guy despaired that "the limited amount of material in the rotunda seems to take the average visitor about 6 minutes to cover." It was not just Guy's curiosity and dry sense of humor that prompted him to write. He was working closely with local boosters to ensure the museum would be a success, and he felt caught between the plodding pace of the Museum Branch and the burgeoning civic pride Maconites had begun to feel for their site of ancient history.

Through all the delay and frustration, the basic modes of representing Ocmulgee's history were coming into focus. Millard Guy lamented that terms like "Mound A," "Mound B," and "Mound C" didn't exactly grab visitors, and from that point forward, the features would be known by the more lyrical "Great Temple Mound," "Lesser Temple Mound," and "Funeral Mound" in park literature. Archaeologists arranged the displays chronologically, from hunting and gathering times through the trading post era, with special emphasis on Mississippian times. The term "Mississippian" had not yet come into vogue among archaeologists, so the site's designers employed "Master Farmers" instead. From a case marked "Living by Hunting," which ran together everything from mammoth to deer, Clovis to atlatl to bow and blowgun, visitors to the first museum might learn that "hunting was hard work." The Archaic period, to 1950s interpreters, was marked by a dietary change. Exhibits referred to the people as "Shellfish Eaters." The presence of pottery heralds the arrival of the "Early Farmers," roughly congruent with today's Woodland designation. Around 900, a race of "Master Farmers" arrived from the Tennessee River region, faced and overcame strong resistance from the Woodland societies they encountered, and brought sweeping change to Ocmulgee. Examples of tools, weapons,

Abbie Rowe photographed many different sites in his work for the National Park Service (he also photographed presidents from Franklin Roosevelt to Lyndon Johnson). This dates to around the time the museum opened, ca. 1950. (Courtesy National Park Service, Ocmulgee National Monument.)

utensils, and ceremonial objects combined with information about diet and funerary practice to make a case for dramatic cultural change in the 1950s display cases. The 1950s-era museum placed about a 250-year gap between the Master Farmers abandoning the large Ocmulgee town and "Early Creeks" building the mounds at the Lamar site. Other key features included the Ocmulgee Old Fields (or trading post) period and a nod to life in the modern Creek Nation. Though the names have changed, and the details have gotten slightly more nuanced in intervening decades, visitors to today's Ocmulgee National Monument are greeted by a very similar division inside the entry hall.

As the museum moved in fits and starts toward its fall 1951 grand opening, the staff was engaged in a publicity blitz. Rangers, administrators, and archaeologists engaged in a whirlwind of activity: giving tours to distinguished guests, talking to school groups, addressing a crowd at Robins Air Force Base, even appearing on a Voice of America radio broadcast. They signed a contract with the Southern Time Table, so that rail line would place Ocmulgee information in hotels and train depots. The Chamber of Commerce also agreed to feature Ocmulgee in a brochure to be distributed in key locations throughout the Southeast. Ocmulgee appeared in American Automobile Association literature as well as in a Standard Oil publication titled *The Scenic South*. Much of the energy was directed close to home, with glowing pieces in the *Macon Telegraph* and a full social schedule for the staff. The Kiwanis club, the Civitan Club, the Chamber of Commerce, the Mercer University Auxiliary, and the Macon Women's Club all hosted events connected with Ocmulgee National Monument.

The Visitor Center was designed by James T. Swanson, who had also directed the Earth Lodge reconstruction project. When the museum officially opened in October 1951, it won deservedly high praise for its architecture, though not everyone was pleased. One critic memorably panned the edifice as "the supremely ugly museum at Georgia's Ocmulgee National Monument." The same critic later opined that the building was a "monstrosity," and that the National Park Service might improve its hideous appearance if it were to "build a mound over it." That lone critic's assessment has proven laughably mistaken over time. The building is at once a triumph of the Art Moderne style (with some later flourishes) and a remarkable homage to the past, represented by the inlaid terra cotta façade called to mind the Lamar Bold Incised style of pottery prevalent at the site.

In October 1951, a sizeable Creek delegation arrived at Ocmulgee. They had traveled all the way from Okmulgee, Oklahoma, and were hyped relentlessly in the local press. Civic clubs from all over Georgia, bands, floats, and all manner of festivities greeted Acee Blue Eagle and the forty-person Creek party when they came to Macon. Robins Air Force Base contributed a float depicting the transition from Mississippian-era warfare to modern military technology.

Young white women, students at Wesleyan College and Mercer University—alternately styled as "brunette beauties" or "brunette lovelies"—competed for the right to be "Boskita Queen" or "Boskita Princess," a reference to the Green Corn, or busk, ceremonies. Maconites looked forward to "one of the most colorful events ever staged in Macon."

Unfortunately, and despite assurances of clear weather, rain washed out the parade and the stickball game and forced the festivities into the City Auditorium. John Davis, principal chief of the Muskogee Creeks and a Baptist minister, addressed the gathering. Highlights included dances and an indoor demonstration of stickball, as well as the aforementioned performance by Acee Blue Eagle. The presence of Native Americans at the 1951 events is documented in a series of striking photographs commissioned by the National Park Service.

Alec Sulphur and Ella Hicks look at Ned Jenkins's diorama depicting the Green Corn ceremony. Creek traditions allowed the people to weather attacks on their identity, whether in the Removal era or in the middle of the twentieth century. (Courtesy National Park Service, Ocmulgee National Monument.)

Some Creeks appear to have been pressed to explain to white reporters the differences between the 1700s and the 1950s. One article, accompanied by a photograph of a young woman named Katie Tulsa wearing turtle-shell rattles and saddle shoes, demonstrates this phenomenon. It notes "the old days when Indian women accepted complete responsibility for setting up the household abode, gathering firewood, preparing food and making clothing, are gone with the last of the buffalo." As a result, Miss Tulsa—described as "pretty, dark-eyed" and in possession of "shapely brown legs"—

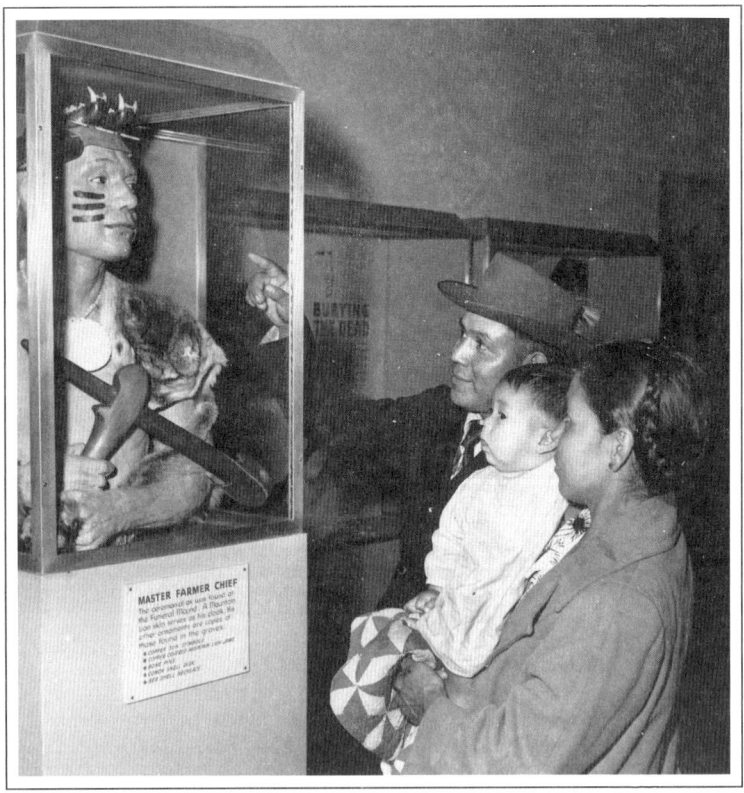

Oklahoma Creeks Louis and Annie Taylor (and young Arnold) enjoyed the Master Farmer statue during their 1951 visit to the museum. (Courtesy National Park Service, Ocmulgee National Monument.)

KEEPING OCMULGEE / 143

Rain forced some of the 1951 festivities inside, but did not dampen the spirits of the thousands of Maconites who gathered to learn about modern Creek culture. Here, members of the Hicks and Asbury families prepare to demonstrate the sport of stickball. (Courtesy National Park Service, Ocmulgee National Monument.)

By the 1950s, Muscogee (Creek) dance blended variations on ancient traditions with the influence of the broader powwow culture. These performers in regalia educated and entertained from the stage of Macon's City Auditorium. Native dancers and makers of regalia have access to a national "feather bank" that allows them to carry on sacred traditions. (Courtesy National Park Service, Ocmulgee National Monument.)

expected any future husband to pull his weight around the house and "mind the baby when she needs a breather." The women's editor at the *Macon News* pointed out, in an article titled "Tepees Swapped for Houses, Braves Lose Independence," that

> many Creek Indians who formerly occupied Georgia…now live on comfortable farms in Oklahoma, and grow corn, wheat, cotton, and potatoes. The women cook on electric stoves, wash their clothes in electric washers and tell stories of former grandeur by electric light rather than the flicker of a campfire. The women help with light field duties as well as do the housework.

Creek marriage ceremonies had changed since the 1700s as well. Instead of contracting a marriage between families, or requiring a man to kill a buck to prove his masculinity, modern Creeks "just go out and get married."

In 1952, a slightly larger Creek delegation returned to Macon, and they were joined this time by a small contingent of Cherokees. The second annual Boskita, as the event was known, benefited from much better weather and high attendance. For weeks beforehand, journalists and sportswriters built excitement for the stickball demonstration, billing the event as "sure to be warlike," for instance. One columnist, practically frothing at the mouth, described the game as "legalized murder and mayhem." Another, after making some relatively balanced comments about U.S. Indian policy ("we haven't yet smoothed all the wrinkles"), argued that the Creeks and Cherokees "couldn't claim to be full-fledged Americans until they can play ball and like it." The event lived up to its violent billing. The Creeks defeated the Cherokees twelve to one, and injuries sent three players, two of them Cherokee, to the local emergency room, where they were treated and released. While doing publicity for the 1952 event, Acee Blue Eagle took pains to remind Maconites that "this is not just a cheap show. It shows racial history and is authentic, colorful, and educational. It shows how the Creeks are keeping alive the folk art of their people." Blue Eagle continued to argue that Ocmulgee could be both a popular tourist attraction and a site of spiritual power for the Creeks.

Beyond the reach of the media spotlight, archaeological work resumed at Ocmulgee in the late 1950s, mainly at the trading post, and under the direction of Carol Irwin (later Mason). She first took an interest in archaeology when she was an undergraduate student of Charles Fairbanks and Hale Smith at Florida State University. Mason would go on to study with James B. Griffin at the University of Michigan and complete her dissertation, *The Archaeology of Ocmulgee Old Fields, Macon, Georgia*, in 1963. The work contributed significantly in a number of areas, most notably in the identification of motifs on pottery and in the identification of various types of European trade goods, including gun parts, bells, and beads associated with the trading post.

Carol Mason (Carol Irwin, at the time of this photograph) added tremendously to our knowledge about Ocmulgee with her fieldwork and scholarship, most notably her dissertation, published as *The Archaeology of Ocmulgee Old Fields, Macon, Georgia*, in 1963. (Courtesy National Park Service, Ocmulgee National Monument.)

While Maconites may have respected Creeks enough to invite them to the museum's opening celebration, their generosity of spirit did not extend to the human remains found at the site. Up through the 1960s, several sets of human remains were on display at Ocmulgee. They had been on display in some form since the pre-Visitor Center days, centered primarily around the excavated trading post and Mound C. Archaeologists uncovered 150 burials at various locations in and around Mound C, and 67 associated with the trading post. One scholar has lamented the fact that particularly acidic soil and slipshod documentation and preservation lessened the scholarly significance of the finds. Most visitors to the site were unconcerned with such matters, however. Early schematic drawings of the trading post site show a handful of burials protected from the elements by burial shelters. Tourists could peer down into the graves. After the enactment of the Native American Graves Protection and Repatriation Act (NAGPRA) in 1990, and in an era that at the very least pays lip service to intercultural understanding, it is difficult to countenance the presence of displays containing human remains. Such practice was practically *de rigueur* in public representations of early Native American history at the time, including sites such as Kolomoki, in southwestern Georgia, and Dickson Mounds, in central Illinois.

In the 1950s, Native Americans returned to Ocmulgee as paid guests of Macon's white city fathers. They were invited to highlight the monument's stunning archaeological importance, but also so that white people from throughout the Southeast might put Macon on their tourist itineraries and spend their money in town. Still, the ambassadors who moved eastward in the 1950s laid the groundwork for less flamboyant and popular, yet perhaps more significant, visits in the 1960s and 1970s.

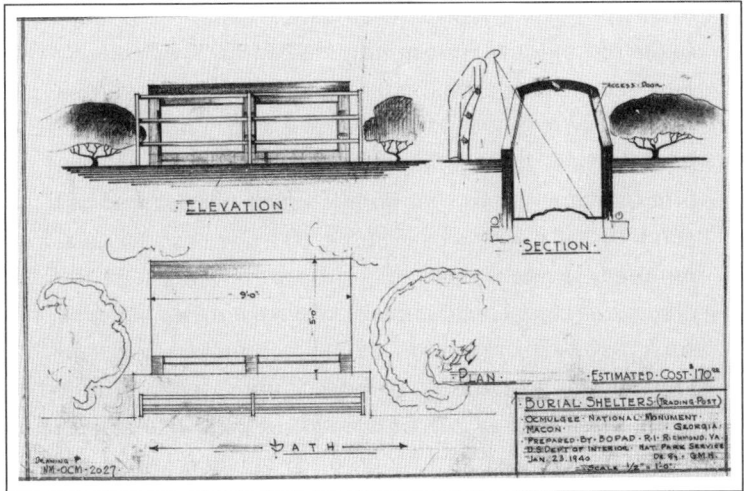

GRAVE DISPLAY SCHEMATIC From the time the park opened until the 1960s, human remains were on display at Ocmulgee. Thankfully, the Native American Graves Protection and Repatriation Act (1990), forbids this practice and ensures that Native communities have a say in the treatment of ancestral remains, grave goods, and sacred objects. (Courtesy National Park Service, Ocmulgee National Monument.)

OCMULGEE FIELD NOTE

COME TO THE TABLE

What the Muscogee Creeks lived on lives on. The grits that warm my winter mornings, the cornbread that my father breaks up into his bowl of buttermilk, the pumpkin in our Thanksgiving pie, the squash in my aunts' casserole – these foods that nourished the first people to make a home along the Ocmulgee and that still nourish their descendants nourish the whole nation. The people native to this place going back to the Mississippians cultivated these comforting foods, generously passing them along to the rest of the human family. Indigenous people taught European colonists how to intercrop corn and beans, how to "hill" corn, how to dry and crack it into hominy, and how to roast it in its shucks. The drying of beans and other summer crops that allowed them to be stored and eaten in the winter was a native practice that colonists imitated. We have these first nations to thank for cornbread, hoe cakes, hush puppies, greens, ginseng, tobacco, sassafras, and peppermint – not to mention the barbecueing and hickory-smoking of meat. Coming to the table to enjoy these gifts of the watershed, we ought to respect and feel gratitude to the people who first sat down here to learn what this river and this earth offered. We ought to be humble enough before the watershed to be good stewards of it, so that our children's children can thrive on its gifts as we have.

"ALL THINGS ARE CONNECTED" OCMULGEE IN THE 1960S AND 1970S

In the late 1950s and early 1960s, a major transportation project posed a serious threat to Ocmulgee. Most business leaders and the mayor shared Carl Vinson's vision for an interstate highway linking Macon and Savannah and running through the monument. (Walter Harris and Cecil Coke were notable exceptions.) As originally planned, I-16 would slice deeply through monument lands between the Great Temple Mound and the Ocmulgee River. The National Park Service seemed to view the route as inevitable and did not offer much resistance. That attitude changed with the arrival of Albert Dillahunty as superintendent in January 1961. Dillahunty bristled at the idea that I-16 as proposed would not disrupt visitors' experiences or the archaeological setting too profoundly. The National Park Service submitted two alternate routes in succession, and both were rejected. Eventually, Vinson, the director of the Bureau of Public Roads, and the director of the National Park Service reached an agreement. The new route would run across Ocmulgee close to the river, ostensibly to minimize the damage to the park's more recognizable features. New archaeological work would also take place before the road went in. The most intensive archaeological work lasted only until 1962, but it laid the foundations for the Southeast Archaeological Center (SEAC), headquartered at Ocmulgee starting in 1966 (the unit would move to Tallahassee in 1972).

The Muscogee (Creek) Nation was reborn in the 1970s. For the first time in a long time, tribal leaders took the reins of their government in a meaningful way. As of 1971, tribal members no longer required presidential approval of their

I-16 CONSTRUCTION Though not nearly as damaging as the railroad cuts of the nineteenth century, the construction of Interstate 16 connecting Savannah and Macon sliced through the monument. Hikers on today's River Trail pass under the highway on their way to the Ocmulgee. (Courtesy National Park Service, Ocmulgee National Monument.)

choice for principal chief. In 1979, tribal members voted a new government into being and created a new national constitution. These momentous times in Creek country were matched by remarkable developments at Ocmulgee. Politicians, diplomats, artists, and people from all walks of life crossed cultural boundaries as local politicians in Middle Georgia forged alliances with Creeks, and Creeks came to Macon and went to work at the monument. To be sure, both Muscogees and whites entered into partnerships for a variety of reasons, but the interaction between the parties was not always free of tension. Still, the 1970s mark a watershed in the modern relationship between Native Americans and the ancient monuments and fields at Ocmulgee.

The Ocmulgee National Monument master plan, produced for the approval of the National Park Service in summer 1972, made multiple references to a modern Creek presence at the monument and indicated a sort of rebirth for the park. The section labeled "management objectives" included as one of its goals a desire to "implement the proposed 'live' demonstrations, arts, and crafts, through cooperation with the Creek Indian tribe and the Ocmulgee Auxiliary Corporation." It called for the immediate hiring of two Creek interpreters, and stressed the deep history of Ocmulgee ("man's occupation of this particular piece of ground for over 10,000 years"), but it also strove to tell a more contemporary tale: "Ocmulgee embraces many stories. One that is potentially exciting has overtones of *here* and *now*. After 150 years, members of the Creek Nation are returning to their homeland to operate a Creek crafts program as a concession in the park's Visitor Center." The concession operation was expected to "sell materials from non-Creek tribes, as well as their own, although all sales items [would] be Indian-made."

The trading post opened to great fanfare in July 1972. Several Creeks who had already moved to Macon (see below) performed. Gerald and Wayne Harjo danced in regalia, Ben

Checotah drummed, and Pinki Webster sang as hundreds of Maconites—perhaps as many as 2,000!—gathered for the momentous occasion. After a brief welcome by Ping Crawford, the park's superintendent since 1969, and a prayer by a local Episcopal priest, Ben Checotah led the crowd in the Pledge of Allegiance. Charles Jones introduced the afternoon's speakers, comprising Principal Chief Claude Cox and Bureau of Indian Affairs and National Park service officials. Recently retired Lakota congressman Ben Reifel, a former BIA administrator, dedicated the trading post; the Creek Nation and the NPS exchanged gifts, and the program concluded with a benediction by Woodrow Haney, a Creek minister. After the official ceremonies drew to a close, singing and dancing resumed. The post was managed by John Moore, a Creek retired master sergeant with three decades' service in the army. He was assisted by Billy Harjo, Dee Anne Sloan, and Addie George, a remarkable Yuchi woman just beginning a long relationship with Ocmulgee National Monument.

In spring 1972, a few weeks before the Trading Post opened, Creeks had begun to move from Oklahoma to Macon. The earliest arrival, George Whiteman, worked at a local body shop and welcomed at least one successive group of Creeks by noting that he was "glad to see some Indians." Other Native people (predominately Creek) who moved that spring included Peggy and Ben Checotah, Lucile and Gerald Harjo, Louis Tulsa, Janice Holata, Dee Anne Sloan, and Ken Yazzie and his wife. Many of these individuals were quite young when they made the move, and the group included some people who had just graduated from high school. They went to work at various jobs around Macon: guiding tours at the monument, working on the maintenance staff there (one park official quipped, "I've got a lot of grass to cut," before noting that the young people would also be engaged in other activities), selling Native-produced crafts at the "trading post," and promoting the monument at an Interstate 75 tourist informa-

TRADING POST OPENING The Trading Post dedication ceremony hints at a blending of National Park Service and various Native American cultures, including the by-the-1970s ubiquitous powwow culture, replete with elaborate buckskin regalia and flowing Plains-style headdresses, such as that worn by Gerald Harjo (foreground). (Courtesy National Park Service, Ocmulgee National Monument.)

MISS ADDIE Addie George, "Miss Addie" to her many friends, appears here at the beginning of a lasting relationship with Ocmulgee National Monument. She and her daughter Valerie visited numerous times. At the time of her death in 2006 (at age 94), she was one of very few people fluent in Yuchi. Miss Addie would probably be pleased that Yuchi children are now being taught the language by elders through the Yuchi Language Project. (Courtesy National Park Service, Ocmulgee National Monument.)

In its 1970s incarnation, the museum's gift shop, or Trading Post, carried items indigenous to the Southeast as well as items that embodied a more generalized "Native American" vibe. (Courtesy National Park Service, Ocmulgee National Monument.)

Dozens of Creeks, and citizens of other Native nations, moved to Macon and worked at Ocmulgee in the 1970s. Gerald Harjo is at far left, and Ben Checotah is at far right. (Courtesy National Park Service, Ocmulgee National Monument.)

tion center. Some attended local colleges including Mercer University and Macon Junior College (today's Middle Georgia State University). The Bureau of Indian Affairs shouldered some of the cost of the project, providing $20,000 to supply the crafts shop and $5,000 for salaries. The BIA also paid for transportation, one month's rent, and some household items.

As with previous efforts in the 1950s, the enthusiasm among Creek people was not universal. During a question and answer session with Charles Jones, a Creek woman named Winey Bell pointed out that "after what the white man has done to my people, I am not interested in going back to Georgia." An editorial in a Tulsa paper reminded white Georgians that they had had their chance with the Creeks—and had blown it: "The Indian refugees conquered a wilderness and took a leading role in the creation of the new state of Oklahoma, then helped nurture it into the space age. No wonder Georgia would like to have back some of her original citizens."

OCMULGEE FIELD NOTE

HURRICANE MATTHEW

August 2016

The August rain breaks seven weeks of drought and wakes me in the wee hours with its guttering in my eaves. Outside at dawn, it speckles me as I pick up the newspaper, making a constellation of cold stars along my shoulders and back. Not all of weather's touches are tender. The city is in the quiet margin of a hurricane, I know, but I let this rain be what it is here where I am, however fierce it is elsewhere. For those near the storm's eye, I offer a wordless prayer.

At Ocmulgee, the air, cooled, feels heavy. The soaked parch of the earth smells like a woman's sweat—the faint mineral odor of a body in use, in toil, salt and damp breaking out in exertion. It's more honest than perfume, this air of candor and met need that has a brackish edge. I think of loam's aroma after the effort of turning it—not that the long-dry ground has remembered itself as loam just yet.

Despite its thirst, the earth has not drawn the rain in. It withholds itself from the water as the water has withheld itself from the ground. Rain with the patience to pool will, in a little while, percolate down into the roots and the fundament. Clays will sip moisture back in and regain their former softness. Sand will lose its crisp edge. The earth and the stormcloud-carried ocean will open to each *other and steep. This drainage will brew itself to a tannic, tepid, nourishing tea.*

I envy the rain and soil this meeting, which must be deeply satisfying—but it isn't so bad to settle for simply being a witness. I am content to sit on the lip of this muddy, ordinary grail.

* * * * *

Ed Johnson, chairman of the Tribal Council of the Creek Nation and a Korean War veteran, said that Creeks were likely to be suspicious about the return, and question the sincerity of it, but would not be openly hostile to it. He went further to say that these were more than just hard feelings toward the city of Macon or Georgia, that the Creeks "question the sincerity of the Bureau of Indian Affairs and even of the tribal leaders. They are afraid of 'promises.' They don't seek the moon, but they do seek a better life and an opportunity to achieve." Ed Johnson, and Principal Chief Claude Cox, both of whom supported the move to Macon, and the Native Americans who eventually moved to Macon, did so for their own reasons.

The Creeks were objects of fascination to white Maconites and were more outspoken and assertive than their predecessors had been in the 1950s. The back-and-forth in the 1970s was indicative of a new era in Native-white relations, and a more forthright nationalism on the part of the Native Americans involved. While some of the Creek delegation were being wined and dined at a banquet in Macon, Charles Jones put his arm around Ben Checotah, in an effort to make the young man feel at ease, and asked if he needed anything. "Yeah. Give us back our land," came Checotah's reply.

Historical wrongs such as dispossession were not the only matters of concern, though. Gerald Harjo had been promised a job at Ocmulgee and assumed his years of college and skills as a ceremonial dancer might qualify him as a guide or

Ben Checotah interpreted Ocmulgee's history for several years in the middle of the 1970s. This image captures the intersection of archaeology, tourism, and modern Native perspectives that has been a hallmark of Ocmulgee since the middle of the twentieth century. (Courtesy National Park Service, Ocmulgee National Monument.)

interpreter. When he found out that he was mainly useful as a lawn mower, he was not pleased: "I could have cut grass in Oklahoma.... I wasn't just some uneducated sonofabitch who couldn't do nothing else but cut grass. I had been to college, Jack! I didn't have to come all the way to Macon, Georgia, to cut grass. I raised hell about it." Harjo worked as a guide for the next three summers, completed an undergraduate degree at Mercer, and then went on to teach history and art at Central High School. His wife, Lucille, who was Choctaw, made and sold pottery at the crafts shop.

Ben and Peggy Checotah seem to have had a slightly more positive experience than Gerald Harjo initially. Ben had been working laying bricks in Oklahoma and had grown weary of it, so the opportunity to move to Macon appealed to him. Peggy Checotah, who was Cherokee, drew a fair amount of attention around town, in part due to her attractiveness. Newspaper articles often mentioned her good looks, and a feature writer for the *Atlanta Journal Constitution* described her as "willowy and regal in appearance, with long dark hair and high cheekbones, giving a classic impression of Indian-princess femininity." She worked at a tourist information center on the interstate north of town. Ben was employed as a tour guide from the beginning and especially enjoyed dismantling the stereotypes held by Macon's schoolchildren. The kids "can't believe I'm a real Indian. One of them asked me where my horse was, and why ... I didn't wear feathers. Another little boy who rode up on his bike said, 'How come you got those kinds of clothes on if you're an Indian,' and then he rode away in disgust."

As summer turned to fall in Macon in 1972, the city geared up to host its first-ever Creek Week, attempting to turn the "Trail of Tears" into a "Trail of Cheers" by honoring returning Creeks and celebrating the county's sesquicentennial. A weeklong celebration of Macon's history, including its Native American past, was to culminate in a three-show run of a historical spectacle. President Nixon himself sent a telegram

TRAIL OF CHEERS MEDALLION Macon held several events in 1972 to promote its historical connection to the Creeks. None was more questionably named than the "Trail of Cheers." (Courtesy National Park Service, Ocmulgee National Monument.)

to the event, congratulating the people of Macon for "their special tribute to Creek Indian influence on modern Macon life." Nixon's telegram read, in part, "Creek Indian Week reminds us of a great heritage which continues to enrich the lives of all our citizens. But more than this, it points to a promising future for the Creek Indian families who return to such a warm welcome to their ancestral home."

The week itself was a bizarre blend of kitsch, faux-tribal traditions, and civic pride and boosterism. There were Girl Scout displays, pottery classes, dances by the Boy Scouts' "Order of the Arrow," and archery demonstrations by Kelly Bell, one of the Creek rangers at Ocmulgee, scheduled opposite "Fast Draw" demonstrations. The film *A Man Called Horse* played for free at a local theater in the evenings. Corn-themed events featured prominently during Creek Week: there was a cornbread sale, as well as a corn-eating contest. Claude Cox served as the grand marshal of a parade on Thursday of Creek Week. The parade route was lined by thousands of Maconites who came out to watch their fellows "play Indian." The parade was thick with thatch huts, tomahawks, and teepees, in addition to the many spectators and participants who turned out in fringed leather and face paint. The winning float, "Along the Ocmulgee," was submitted by a group that called itself the Indian Lore Society of Hawkinsville. It featured a man and woman "dressed as Indians," as well as a thatch-roofed house, arrowheads, and a beaver.

The same Thursday that the parade snaked through downtown Macon, Gerald Harjo appeared in the local paper. He was interviewed about a particularly gruesome painting he was working on in which Native Americans are shot and collapse to the ground, "their heads in puddles of blood." Harjo explained, "I felt bad, being mistreated, the racial side. So I created this picture and that's it." The artist followed immediately by noting that "Macon is great. Ever since we've been here we've been treated kind of special."

One of the highlights of 1972's "Creek Week," intended to promote Macon's historical connection to the Muscogee (Creek) Nation, was a parade. Floats and pageants allowed non-Natives to "play Indian," a phenomenon deeply ingrained in American identity. (Courtesy National Park Service, Ocmulgee National Monument.)

Creek Week culminated in a brief run of "Return of the Creeks," billed as an "Indian Symphonic Drama." The production was to tie everything together and relate it to the past. Perhaps not surprisingly for a play containing a cast of around 300 amateur actors, "Return of the Creeks" did not impress local drama critics. Some of the dialogue won praise as "excellent and moving," such as the moment "a Creek chief" declared, "Every hope is ended. Once I the warrior, but I cannot animate the dead." The end of the show bred confusion, as children dressed like Indians twirled red, white, and blue streamers on stage, followed by the playing of the "Star-Spangled Banner." Two Creeks appeared in the show, though they did not have speaking parts. The writer and director decided not to include any lengthy treatment of Indian removal in the pageant because they deemed it "too ugly."

The aftermath of Creek Week was unpleasant on multiple fronts. The event cost much more than planned, and feuding erupted over who should foot the bill. Unfortunately, Ocmulgee National Monument, and the Creeks who had come to be associated with it, suffered. The site also weathered a period of administrative turmoil and conflict with the city of Macon. Visits to Ocmulgee dropped precipitously, and the gift shop and associated Indian craft shop were forced to close. Some Creeks who worked at the monument would later describe feeling used. Almost all would leave Georgia, though some living history programs and artist-in-residence initiatives would continue to bring Native Americans from various nations together at Ocmulgee later in the 1970s.

In the 1970s, park literature and signage adopted the motto "All Things Are Connected," from a speech allegedly delivered by Chief Seattle (Sealth) to mark the arrival of a U.S. delegation to the Pacific Northwest. Seattle did, in fact, make a speech on that occasion, but it neither contained the ringing phrase "all things are connected" nor did it focus on the environment. Ted Perry, a white screenwriter and later a film professor, composed the speech for a 1970s made-for-television movie, and the words ended up being attributed to Seattle. To his credit, Perry has tried to disentangle his version from the speech Seattle actually delivered, but the famous phrase has taken on a life of its own.

OCMULGEE FIELD POEM

SWALLOW

Matthew 6:26

The mud nests that edge the eave of the bridge
    seem simple until I watch a male, his beak a split seed,
ferry clay from upstream for a long May morning.
    He daubs it under the road mouthful by mouthful,
building without hands a perfect bowl. By noon,
    he has begun to narrow it into a half-bottle.
He can spare four quick flits to pluck gnats from the air.
    To drink, he folds his wings, skims a sip of river,
then flares back into flight, skipping me like a flat chip
    of feldspar off the current's glinting warble.
Birds do sow. Birds reap. He eats, drinks, and lives for birth.
    His mate settles, chepping. He spackles her in with earth.

* * * * *

STABILITY, EXPANSION, AND REVITALIZATION THE 1980S AND 1990S

Ocmulgee was able to move beyond the tumult of the late 1970s thanks to steady leadership. The park also benefited mightily from a strengthened relationship with the Muscogee (Creek) Nation. This renewed alliance, and Ocmulgee itself, came under serious pressure in the 1980s and 1990s as a proposed road project threatened the monument and associated

Creek lands. In the 1990s, one of the modern park's most significant and enduring traditions was reborn, with the annual Ocmulgee Indian Celebration taking the place formerly occupied by the 1970s and early 1950s festivities.

Sibbald Smith began his stint as superintendent in December 1979. He worked diligently to streamline the park's operations in an era of federal austerity, at least as far as National Parks were concerned, and to rebuild relationships with the surrounding community. There are plenty of examples, but one that stands out is the collaboration between Smith and Aaron Hyatt (president of Macon College, today's Middle Georgia State University), among others, on a steering committee that guided the planning for Ocmulgee's fiftieth anniversary in 1986. The highlights included a reunion of the CCC workers who had labored so intensively in the 1930s to lay the groundwork for the modern park. He also teamed with the Ocmulgee National Monument Association, a community group charged with raising funds and awareness to support new initiatives and to improve outreach. Alan Marsh, who began working at Ocmulgee as a student volunteer in the mid-1980s, would continue to serve the site as in a variety of capacities, including writing an invaluable 1986 administrative history of the monument. Marsh would eventually move on to work as a cultural resources specialist at Andersonville, but he has returned to serve as the emcee of the Ocmulgee Indian Celebration in recent years.

Ocmulgee National Monument acquired new property in 1991 when it added Drake's Field, a complex of ballfields used by Bibb Manufacturing Company employees and their families earlier in the twentieth century. The area still awaits a full archaeological investigation, but ground-penetrating radar studies carried out by Daniel Bigman in 2010 indicate that the settlements that surrounded the trading post may have been larger and stretched farther to the west than previously assumed. In 1997, the park and some surrounding areas gained recognition as the first Traditional Cultural Property (TCP) east of the Mississippi River, though the circumstances leading up to that designation were unpleasant to say the least. For some time, regional transportation authorities had toyed with the idea of a Fall Line Freeway that would run from Columbus to Augusta. As those plans became more clearly defined in the 1990s, it appeared as though the proposed route through Macon, known as the Eisenhower Parkway Extension, would run perilously close to the boundaries of Ocmulgee National Monument and risk damaging sacred lands and as-yet-undocumented archaeological sites. Local activists, including the dentist Lindsay "Doc" Holliday, sprang into action to pressure officials to change the route. Muscogee Creeks and other Native nations weighed in against the project as well. Even after TCP status was achieved, granting the area

EISENHOWER PARKWAY EXTENSION PROTEST Local activists partnered with representatives from various Southeastern Indian nations to protest the possibility of building the Eisenhower Parkway Extension in the 1990s. The planned road did, at least, result in the designation of a Traditional Cultural Property, which adds a layer of protection for lands near Ocmulgee. (Courtesy National Park Service, Ocmulgee National Monument.)

an extra layer of protection, road planners continued to eye possible routes through it. Activist pressure, combined with the economic downturn of the early 2000s, appears to have finally stopped consideration of the offending route.

Every September since 1991, dozens of Native American performers, crafters, and storytellers have come to Ocmulgee to take part in the Ocmulgee Indian Celebration. Many, though by no means all, of the participants represent Southeastern nations. While the size of the Creek delegation varies from year to year, the people's continued presence at the event signifies their lasting commitment to Ocmulgee. The three-day affair includes some elements of broader powwow culture as well as performances specific to the Southeast. It also provides

The modern Ocmulgee Indian Celebration began in 1991, though it has parallels in the events of the 1970s and 1950s. Thousands of visitors flock to Ocmulgee in the third week of September each year, and dozens of Native vendors and performers from various nations enlighten and entertain them. (Photograph by Maryann Bates, courtesy of the Ocmulgee National Monument Association.)

opportunities for Native vendors to reach a market that they might otherwise find difficult to access. In recent years, as many as 20,000 guests have attended the celebration, making it one of Macon's largest events and one of the largest Native gatherings in the South. The event has garnered recognition in the regional tourist trade as one of the "Top Twenty Events in the Southeast." This success owes a great deal to the efforts of Sylvia Flowers, a ranger who worked tirelessly to connect Ocmulgee to its Creek past in a variety of ways, including a Cultural Ambassadors program that brought Native speakers to Macon in the mid-1990s.

Interactions between the Muscogee (Creek) Nation and Ocmulgee are not limited to each September's celebra-

In many years, Native people from Oklahoma demonstrate the venerable sport of stickball to educate and thrill visitors to the Ocmulgee Indian Celebration. (Photograph by Sharman Ayoub, courtesy of the Ocmulgee National Monument Association.)

tion. In fact, as an entity of the federal government, Ocmulgee National Monument is bound by NAGPRA to consult with the nation (among other concerned parties) whenever archaeological work is undertaken in the park. Native consultants worked closely with Ocmulgee over the course of the 1990s to make sure Creek remains and sacred objects were handled in a culturally appropriate, respectful way. A lot of these doings were behind the scenes, but a sign near the steps to the Great Temple Mound is a visible reminder to visitors that modern

Native American veterans of the United States Armed Forces are accorded high honors at powwows and similar events around the country. The Muscogee (Creek) Nation Honor Guard is a fixture at the annual celebration. Muscogee servicemen Ernest Childers and Ernest Evans are two of the twenty-nine Native Americans who have received the Congressional Medal of Honor. During the First World War, Choctaw infantrymen used their native language to outwit German code breakers. These original Choctaw Code Talkers were Solomon Louis, Mitchell Bobb, Ben Carterby, Robert Taylor, Jeff Nelson, Pete Maytubby, James Edwards, and Calvin Wilson. At the time, they were ineligible for U.S. citizenship and Choctaw children were forbidden to speak the language in government-run boarding schools. (Photograph by Maryann Bates, courtesy of the Ocmulgee National Monument Association.)

Creeks hold the parcel of land sacred, and that guests should comport themselves accordingly. The monument's relationship with the Muscogee (Creek) Nation, rejuvenated in the 1990s, would grow even stronger in the years to come.

PART 7

OCMULGEE TO OKMULGEE

This book's seven parts pay tribute to the significance of the number seven in Creek cosmology. According to some variants of that cosmology, Creeks recognize seven directions. In addition to the four cardinal directions, these include skyward, earthward, and inward. One Creek term for this is *puyvfekcv* (pronounced "boea fikcha"), which refers to the continuum of energy, or "fire within spirit," flowing through all things. In addition to being roughly laid out along the cardinal directions, it might be said that Ocmulgee's planners dug earthward to project their monuments skyward. There is no doubt that many generations of Creeks have found great power, even a ceremonial center of the nation, in the site.

In 2012, in front of perhaps the largest delegation of Creeks at Ocmulgee since removal, Muscogee (Creek) Nation principal Chief George Tiger told a story that had been passed down through the generations of Creeks in Oklahoma, "It is said that our forefathers and foremothers, as they were preparing to make a trip to an unknown land and an unknown place, had a vision, and that vision was that someday the following generations would come back to their motherland, and be a part of something." In another section of the moving address, Tiger added that "when they come back to the original homelands, they'll be much stronger." Today, there is little

Principal Chief George Tiger addresses a large crowd gathered at the beginning of the 2012 Ocmulgee to Okmulgee bike ride. (Courtesy Muscogee [Creek] Nation, Cultural Preservation Office.)

Creek citizens John Beaver, then the director of the Creek Cultural Center and Museum, and Andrew "Raymond" Lowe, a Vietnam veteran, rode from Ocmulgee National Monument to Okmulgee, Oklahoma, in the summer of 2012. A handful of local cyclists accompanied them on the starting leg of the journey. (Muscogee [Creek] Nation, Cultural Preservation Office.)

doubt that the Muscogee (Creek) Nation is strong. It counts nearly 80,000 enrolled citizens, and touts a rejuvenated language program (approximately ten percent of Muscogee Nation citizens are fluent speakers). The nation is working toward economic development and cultural revitalization on a number of fronts.

Ocmulgee National Monument is strong and getting stronger as well, and the connection between the Creeks and Ocmulgee continues to flourish in the twenty-first century. The Museum and Visitor Center underwent a thorough redesign in the 2000s, and the Muscogee (Creek) Nation consulted at various steps in the process. The result was nothing short of breathtaking. The museum had always been a beautiful showcase for artifacts, but the redesign, completed in 2009, approached the site's history and interpretation from several

Building on the momentum established in prior decades, and hearkening back to ancient traditions, the Muscogee (Creek) Nation constructed a new tribal complex in Okmulgee, Oklahoma, in the 1970s and called it "The Mound." The Mound houses tribal offices and the national court and council chambers. (Photograph by Matthew Jennings.)

different angles. There were interactive features, in which visitors could take seats in a model of the Earth Lodge, apply paddle designs to pots, or lift baskets of clay as if they were about to carry them to the top of a mound. Videos demonstrating flint-knapping and pottery were joined by 1950s footage showing a wide-ranging stickball game in Oklahoma. There was an updated display highlighting the tools and practices of archaeology in the 1930s and 1940s, a nod to Ocmulgee's importance to the discipline or archaeology. New wall panels treated the relationship between Macon's early history and the site, and told the story of Creek Removal (as traumatic, if less well-known, than that of the Cherokee Trail of Tears). A large display, with multiple video contributions, highlighted the return of Muskogee people (and other Native Americans) to the site since the 1990s rebirth of the Ocmulgee Indian Celebration. What's more, the new display also contained a large photograph of the National Council and Supreme Court building in Okmulgee, Oklahoma, known informally as "The Mound," in reference to the architecture of Ocmulgee, among other sites. As hinted at in the previous chapter, Ocmulgee's profile as a regional tourist attraction continued to rise in the early twenty-first century. The monument also made waves in the art world when internationally renowned Cheyenne/Arapaho artist Hock E Aye Vi Edgar Heap of Birds used it as the inspiration for an installation at the Atlanta College of Art and on the streets of midtown Atlanta. Heap of Birds is known for creating pieces that call attention to Native American history and persistence in places where it might otherwise go overlooked. For *Ocmulgee,* the artist graced the gallery space with two large truncated pyramids reminiscent of the Great and Lesser Temple Mounds. The sides of the structures featured Mississippian symbols. Heap of Birds also transformed the nearby streetscape with forty-eight steel panels styled after street signs. Instead of mundane warnings about parking, the signs confronted viewers with phrases such as "Were You

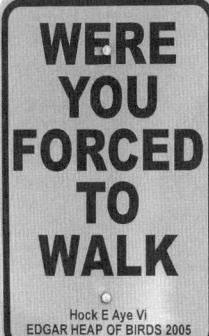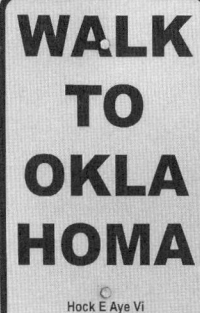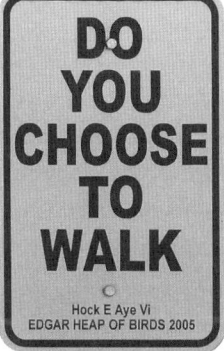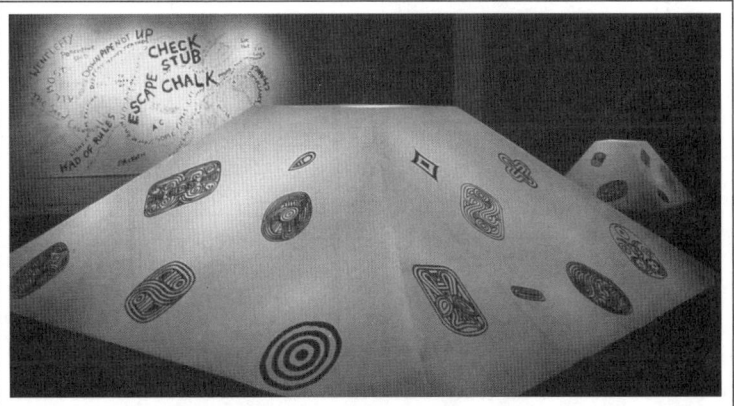

Cheyenne/Arapaho artist Hock E Aye Vi / Edgar Heap of Birds titled his evocative 2005 Atlanta installation Ocmulgee in reference to the national monument. (Used with permission of the artist.)

Forced to Walk" and "Walk to Oklahoma." The accompanying artist's statement read, in part, "The spirits of Ocmulgee return to usher forth these supportive notions of walking and astronomical renewal. They serve as reminders of the revered ways of the past, which offer respect to the star-lit heavenly bodies above and equal treatment of those human bodies we share."

George Tiger's 2012 appearance at Ocmulgee was one facet of a signal event in Ocmulgee's long history. John Beaver, at that time the director of the Muscogee (Creek) Nation Museum and Cultural Center, envisioned a bicycle trip from Ocmulgee in Georgia to Okmulgee, Oklahoma, retracing the path followed by nineteenth-century Creeks as they were driven from the Southeast. Dozens of Creek dignitaries, including Principal Chief Tiger, the second chief, the speaker of the national council, and several elders traveled to Ocmulgee for the occasion in 2012. The event was at once celebratory and solemn. Quiet prayers and hymns offered in Muskogee accompanied the powerful words of Chief Tiger. A handful of local cyclists turned out to ride the first leg of the trip. Andrew "Raymond" Lowe, a Creek citizen and Vietnam veteran, decided to join the ride, too. Beaver and Lowe, along with Justin Giles in the support vehicle, spent the next month on the road. They stopped at key points in the Southeast to run educational programs, and they arrived in Oklahoma in time for the Muscogee (Creek) Nation Festival in June.

At various points in the recent past, Ocmulgee National Monument has inched toward recognition as a National Historical Park and a name change. At first glance, the difference between a National Monument and a National Historical Park may seem cosmetic, but the change would bring real benefits in terms of increased federal funding. And a move from "Ocmulgee National Monument" to "Ocmulgee Mounds National Historical Park" would be a nice blend of the language by which the site is known in National Park Service literature and the way people from the surrounding area refer to it. To this day, many Maconites refer to Ocmulgee simply as "the Indian Mounds." Beyond the change in terminology, the proposed legislation would also allow for a dramatic expansion of the park from its current size, around 700 acres, to approximately 2800 acres. The larger park would join the main unit to the Lamar site and cover a sizable portion of the Traditional Cultural Property. The measure garnered bipartisan support in Georgia and passed the U.S. House of Representatives in 2016, only to fall victim to legislative wrangling at the end of a frantic Senate session. As of this writing, the bill has once again passed the House, though its fate in the Senate remains unclear. These are anxious times for Ocmulgee. Unlike some previous instances, the surrounding community is firmly in Ocmulgee's corner this time around. The Ocmulgee National Park and Preserve Initiative has brought together outdoors enthusiasts, preservationists, and community activists of various stripes to support the creation of a vast preserve attached to the new park. The Muscogee (Creek) Nation and other Native entities have passed resolutions of support, and the National Parks Conservation Association has taken on a leading advocacy role as well. Historians are not necessarily known for their ability to predict the future, but Ocmulgee's future certainly appears promising from this vantage point.

Each era of Ocmulgee's history has left its mark on the site. Some of these marks are easy to discern. Huge clay pyramids and noisy freight trains are kind of hard to miss, after all. Other marks are not quite as apparent. The traces of the first inhabitants took painstaking archaeological work—and good luck—to find. Some of Ocmulgee's story can be found in libraries and archives, but other parts remain the province of Creek healers and elders. Truly majestic events took place in and around the site, but Ocmulgee has also witnessed tragedy and trauma. Each layer of history has added to the story of Ocmulgee.

One fact endures: over the years, many people have sensed great power in the site, or imbued the site with power, or drawn power from the site. Ocmulgee need not mean the same thing to all people, but it has meant *something* to lot of people for a long time. All signs indicate that it will continue to do so in the future.

OCMULGEE FIELD POEM

MUSKOGEE STOMP DANCE

1. Ocmulgee National Monument, Macon, GA

Each September, near the mounds along the Ocmulgee River,
this dance of percussive prayer and held hands passes
its human chain close by me in a rhythm and motion
that belong here. Elder-led, the linked dancers wind
into a gradually tightening spiral. A white crowd
watches. Over the creek, inside a grassy rise,
the rebuilt council house, its clay floor
still firm after seven centuries, still
centered on the sacred fire, stands.
Around that fire, a similar spiral
once circled. In the morning air,
turtle-shell shakers around
the women's ankles make
the old music and
the Muskogee
move to it.

2. Okmulgee, Oklahoma

On the Muskogee Nation site, a mekko remembers boyhood
in a newer Okmulgee. Growing up near the sacred grounds,
he heard the turtle shells shake and his aunts' songs rise,
drawing him to this dance that made its own music.
Because he was the son of an evangelist, a pastor
bringing others to baptism, the boy could listen
only from a distance. He followed his father,
not his father's fathers, not his aunts. He
heard his heritage, close, out of reach.
Then his father changed. He heard,
too, and turned back to the dances.
I don't want to call it loss of faith,
the mekko says. His pastor father
opened his mother's old camp to
dancing and to Green Corn.
It's just in your blood,
the mekko says. *It's
a homecoming.*

3. Somewhere Between

Faith will rise from a place. Give you a place. Hold you in place.
Okmulgee and Ocmulgee each hold faith. Both are ground
reverence grows from. The music, the feet, the motion—
sure as a stomp-dance step against ancestral ground—
wind in a spiral, gathering the people in song.
Selves lost, they become one circle
to celebrate the creation's rebirth.
Among them, low to the grass,
the children's feet touch
the old, old
earth.

SOURCES AND FURTHER READING

Since many of the works listed below cover multiple phases of Ocmulgee's history, rather than listing them multiple times, we have cited them in the sections where they had the greatest influence.

PART 1

INTRODUCTION (AND SOME GENERAL WORKS)

Archeologist's Monthly Reports, Ocmulgee National Monument Curatorial Department. Ocmulgee National Monument.

Bartram, William. *The Travels of William Bartram.* Francis Harper's Naturalist Edition. Athens: University of Georgia Press, 1998. First published 1958. Quotation is from pg. 35.

Chaudhuri, Jean and Joyotpaul. *A Sacred Path: The Way of the Muscogee Creeks.* Los Angeles: UCLA American Indian Studies Center, 2001.

Fairbanks, Charles H. *Archeology of the Funeral Mound, Ocmulgee National Monument, Georgia.* Tuscaloosa: University of Alabama Press, 2003. First published 1956.

Hally, David, ed. *Ocmulgee Archaeology, 1936–1986.* Athens: University of Georgia Press, 1994. See individual listings below for specific chapters referenced.

Jennings, Matthew. *Ocmulgee National Monument.* Images of America Series. Charleston: Arcadia Publishing, 2015.

Jones, Charles Colcock, Jr. *Antiquities of the Southern Indians, Particularly of the Georgia Tribes.* New York: D. Appleton, 1873.

Lewis, David, Jr., and Ann T. Jordan. *Creek Indian Medicine Ways: The Enduring Power of Mvskoke Religion.* Albuquerque: University of New Mexico Press, 2002.

Marsh, Alan. *Ocmulgee National Monument: An Administrative History.* Washington, DC: National Park Service, 1982.

Martin, Jack B., and Margaret McKane Mauldin. *A Dictionary of Creek/Muskogee.* Lincoln: University of Nebraska Press, 2004.

Mereness, Newton D. "Ranger's Report of Travels with General Oglethorpe." In *Travels in the American Colonies*, 215–36. New York: Macmillan, 1916.

Pope, G. D., Jr. *Ocmulgee.* National Park Service Historical Handbook No. 24. Washington, DC: Government Printing Office, 1956.

Walker, John W. "A Brief History of Ocmulgee Archaeology." In *Ocmulgee Archaeology, 1936–1986*, edited by David Hally, 15–35. Athens: University of Georgia Press, 1994.

Wheeler, Beth J. *Ocmulgee National Monument: Cultural Landscape Report.* Washington, DC: National Park Service, 2007.

White, Max E. *The Archaeology and History of the Native Georgia Tribes.* Gainesville: University Press of Florida, 2002.

Wickman, Patricia Riles. *The Tree That Bends: Discourse, Power, and the Survival of the Maskókî People.* Tuscaloosa: University of Alabama Press, 1999.

PART 2

ARRIVING AND FORGING SOCIETIES

Anderson, David G. and Kenneth E. Sassaman. *The Paleoindian and Early Archaic Southeast.* Tuscaloosa: University of Alabama Press, 1996.

Anderson, David G., R. Jerald Ledbetter, and Lisa O'Steen. *Paleoindian Period Archaeology of Georgia.* University of Georgia Laboratory of Archaeology Series 28 (October 1990).

———, and Robert C. Mainfort, Jr., eds. *The Woodland Southeast.* Tuscaloosa: University of Alabama Press, 2002.

Hally, David, et. al. "Swift Creek Vessel Forms and Vessel Assemblages in Northern and Central Georgia." *Early Georgia* 43: 1& 2 (Spring 2015) 41-86.

Love, Sara, and Daniel P. Bigman. "Late Archaic Occupations at Ocmulgee." Paper delievered at Southeastern Archaeological Conference, 2014. Greenville, South Carolina.

Meltzer, David J. *First Peoples in a New World: Colonizing Ice Age America*. Berkeley: University of California Press, 2009.

Sassaman, Kenneth E. *The Eastern Archaic, Historicized*. Lanham, MD: Altamira Press, 2010.

Schmidt, Peter R. and Stephen A. Mrozowski, eds. *The Death of Prehistory*. Oxford: Oxford University Press, 2013.

Smallwood, Ashley M., David G. Anderson, and R. Jerald Ledbetter. "Recent Paleoindian Research in Georgia: Evidence and Implications." In *Ocmulgee Archaeology: New Perspectives from Central Georgia*, edited by Daniel P. Bigman. Athens: University of Georgia Press, forthcoming.

Williams, Mark. *A World Engraved: Archaeology of the Swift Creek Culture*. Tuscaloosa: University of Alabama Press, 1998.

Williams, Stephen, ed. *The Waring Papers: The Collected Works of Antonio J. Waring, Jr*. Cambridge, MA: The Peabody Museum, Harvard University, 1968.

PART 3

MAKING MONUMENTS

Bigman, Daniel P. "An Early Mississippian Settlement History of Ocmulgee." Ph.D. dissertation, University of Georgia, 2012.

———, and Adam King. "New Radio-Carbon Dates for Ocmulgee's Early Mississippian Beginning." Paper delivered at Southeastern Archaeological Conference 2014. Greenville, South Carolina.

Bowne, Eric E. *Mound Sites of the Ancient South: A Guide to the Mississippian Chiefdoms*. Athens: University of Georgia Press, 2013.

Chappell, Sally A. Kitt. *Cahokia: Mirror of the Cosmos*. Chicago: University of Chicago Press, 2002.

Green, Lillian. "Mossy Oak Revisited: A Case Study in Mississippian Ceramics." M. A. Thesis, Georgia State University, 2014.

Knight, Vernon James, Jr. "Symbolism of Mississippian Mounds." In *Powhatan's Mantle: Indians in the Colonial Southeast*, edited by Gregory A. Waselkov et al. Lincoln: University of Nebraska Press, 2006. First published 1989.

Miller, Jay. *Ancestral Mounds: Vitality and Volatility of Native America*. Lincoln: University of Nebraska Press, 2015.

Pauketat, Timothy R. *Ancient Cahokia and the Mississippians*. Cambridge: Cambridge University Press, 2004.

———. *Chiefdoms and Other Archaeological Delusions*. Lanham, MD: AltaMira Press, 2007.

Reilly, F. Kent, III, and James F. Garber, eds. *Ancient Objects and Sacred Realms: Interpretations of Mississippian Iconography*. Austin: University of Texas Press, 2007.

Steere, Benjamin. *The Archaeology of Houses and Households in the Native Southeast*. Tuscaloosa: University of Alabama Press, 2012.

Townsend, Robert F., ed. *Hero, Hawk, and Open Hand: American Indian Art of the Ancient Midwest and South*. New Haven: Yale University Press, 2004.

Williams, Mark. *Lamar Revisited: 1996 Test Excavations at the Lamar Site (9Bi2)*. Lamar Institute Publication no. 43. Savannah: Lamar Institute, 1999.

———, and Gary Shapiro, eds. *Lamar Archaeology: Mississippian Chiefdoms in the Deep South*. Tuscaloosa: University of Alabama Press, 1990.

Williams, Stephen. *Fantastic Archaeology: The Wild Side of North American Prehistory*. Philadelphia: University of Pennsylvania Press, 1991.

PART 4

SITTING DOWN

Anderson, David G. *The Savannah River Chiefdoms: Political Change in the Late Prehistoric Southeast*. Tuscaloosa: University of Alabama Press, 1994.

Beck, Robin. *Chiefdoms, Collapse, and Coalescence in the Early American South*. Cambridge: Cambridge University Press, 2013.

Boyd, Mark F., Hale G. Smith, and John W. Griffin, eds. *Here They Once Stood: The Tragic End of the Apalachee Missions*. Gainesville: University of Florida Press, 1951.

Braund, Kathryn E. Holland. *Deerskins and Duffels: Creek Indian Trade with Anglo-America, 1685–1815*. Lincoln: University of Nebraska Press, 1993.

Clayton, Lawrence A., Vernon James Knight, Jr., and Edward C. Moore, eds. *The De Soto Chronicles: The Expedition of Hernando de Soto to North America in 1539–1543*. Tuscaloosa: University of Alabama Press, 1993.

Corkran, David H. *The Creek Frontier, 1540–1783*. Norman: University of Oklahoma Press, 1967.

Cornelison, John, Jessica McNeil, and Daniel Bigman. "New Understanding of the Historic Creek Town Size and Layouts at Ocmulgee." Paper delivered at Southeastern Archaeological Conference 2014. Greenville, South Carolina.

Crane, Verner W. *The Southern Frontier, 1670–1732*. New York: W. W. Norton, 1981. First published 1928.

Ethridge, Robbie. *From Chicaza to Chickasaw: The European Invasion and the Transformation of the Mississippian World, 1540–1715*. Chapel Hill: University of North Carolina Press, 2010.

———, and Sheri M. Shuck-Hall. *Mapping the Mississippian Shatter Zone: The Colonial Indian Slave Trade and Regional Instability in the America South*. Lincoln: University of Nebraska Press, 2009.

———, and Charles Hudson, eds. *The Transformation of the Southeastern Indians, 1540–1760*. Jackson: University Press of Mississippi, 2002.

Gallay, Alan. *The Indian Slave Trade: The Rise of the English Empire in the American South, 1670–1732*. New Haven: Yale University Press, 2002.

Hahn, Steven C. *The Invention of the Creek Nation, 1670–1763*. Lincoln: University of Nebraska Press, 2004.

Hall, Joseph M., Jr. *Zamumo's Gifts: Indian-European Exchange in the Colonial Southeast*. Philadelphia: University of Pennsylvania Press, 2009.

Hammock, Stephen A. "The Archaeology of the Ochese Creek Indians of the Ocmulgee River Valley, Georgia, A.D. 1680–1715." D. Phil Thesis in progress. University of Oxford, Oxford U.K. Used with permission.

Hann, John H. *The Native American World Beyond Apalachee: West Florida and the Chattahoochee Valley*. Gainesville: University Press of Florida, 2006.

Hudson, Charles. *Knights of Spain, Warriors of the Sun: Hernando de Soto and the South's Ancient Chiefdoms.* Athens: University of Georgia Press, 1997.

———, and Carmen Chaves Tesser, eds. *The Forgotten Centuries: Indians and Europeans in the American South, 1521–1704.* Athens: University of Georgia Press, 1994.

Jennings, Matthew. *New Worlds of Violence: Cultures and Conquests in the Early American Southeast.* Knoxville: University of Tennessee Press, 2011.

Juricek, John T. *Colonial Georgia and the Creeks: Anglo-Indian Diplomacy on the Southern Frontier, 1733–1763.* Gainesville: University Press of Florida, 2010.

Kelton, Paul. *Epidemics and Enslavement: Biological Catastrophe in the Native Southeast, 1492–1715.* Lincoln: University of Nebraska Press, 2007.

Mason, Carol I. *The Archaeology of Ocmulgee Old Fields, Macon, Georgia.* Tuscaloosa: University of Alabama Press, 2005.

McEwan, Bonnie G., ed. *Indians of the Greater Southeast: Historical Archaeology and Ethnohistory.* Gainesville: University Press of Florida, 2000.

———. *The Spanish Missions of La Florida.* Gainesville: University Press of Florida, 1993.

Paulett, Robert. *An Empire of Small Places: Mapping the Southeastern Anglo-Indian Trade, 1732–1795.* Athens: University of Georgia Press, 2012.

Ramsey, William L. *The Yamasee War: A Study of Culture, Economy, and Conflict in the Colonial South.* Lincoln: University of Nebraska Press, 2008.

Snyder, Christina. *Slavery in Indian Country: The Changing Face of Captivity in Early America.* Cambridge: Harvard University Press, 2010.

Swanton, John R. *The Indians of the Southeastern United States.* Washington, DC: Smithsonian Institution Press, 1979. First published 1946.

Wesson, Cameron B., and Mark A. Rees, eds. *Between Contacts and Colonies: Archaeological Perspectives on the Protohistoric Southeast.* Tuscaloosa: University of Alabama Press, 2002.

Worth, John. *The Struggle for the Georgia Coast.* Tuscaloosa: University of Alabama Press, 2007. First published 1995.

Wright, J. Leitch. *The Only Land They Knew: American Indians in the Old South*. Lincoln: University of Nebraska Press, 1999. First published 1981.

PART 5
LOSING AND FINDING OCMULGEE

Many historical documents quoted in this chapter (specifically the "Creek Indian file" and the "Indian Depredations" volumes) can be found in the Georgia Department of Archives and History in Morrow, Georgia. Documents pertaining to the Central of Georgia Railroad are housed in the Georgia Historical Society in Savannah. Labor information for the Central of Georgia came from the Middle Georgia Archives, Washington Memorial Library, Macon.

Adair, James. *The History of the American Indians; Particularly Those Nations Adjoining to the Missisippi* [sic] *East and West Florida, Georgia, South and North Carolina, and Virginia*. London, 1775. Quoted material is from 2012 reprint of original.

Dowd, Gregory Evans. *A Spirited Resistance: The North American Indian Struggle for Unity, 1745–1815*. Baltimore: Johns Hopkins University Press, 1992.

Ethridge, Robbie. *Creek Country: The Creek Indians and Their World*. Chapel Hill: University of North Carolina Press, 2003.

Elliott, Daniel T. *Fort Hawkins History and Archaeology*. Lamar Institute Publication no. 107. Savannah: The Lamar Institute, 2007.

Foster, H. Thomas II. *Archaeology of the Lower Muskogee Creek Indians, 1715–1836*. Tuscaloosa: University of Alabama Press, 2007.

——, ed. *The Collected Works of Benjamin Hawkins, 1796–1810*. Tuscaloosa: University of Alabama Press, 2003.

Frank, Andrew. *Creeks and Southerners: Biculturalism on the Early American Frontier*. Lincoln: University of Nebraska Press, 2005.

Green, Michael D. *The Politics of Indian Removal: Creek Government and Society in Crisis*. Lincoln: University of Nebraska Press, 1985.

Haveman, Christopher D. *Rivers of Sand: Creek Indian Emigration, Relocation, and Ethnic Cleansing in the American South*. Lincoln: University of Nebraska Press, 2016.

Iobst, Walter. *Civil War Macon*. Macon: Mercer University Press, 1999.

Jones, Charles Colcock, Jr. *Monumental Remains of Georgia*. Savannah: John M. Cooper and Company, 1861. Quoted material comes from manuscript copy in the University of Georgia's Richard Russell Special Collections Library.

Kelly, Arthur. *A Preliminary Report on Archaeological Explorations at Macon, Georgia*. Bulletin No. 119, Bureau of American Ethnology. Washington, DC: Government Printing Office, 1938.

Lyon, Edwin A. *A New Deal for Southeastern Archaeology*. Tuscaloosa: University of Alabama Press, 1996.

Martin, Joel W. *A Sacred Revolt: The Muskogees' Struggle for a New World*. Boston: Beacon Press, 1991.

Saunt, Claudio. *A New Order of Things: Property, Power, and the Transformation of the Creek Indians, 1733–1816*. Cambridge: Cambridge University Press, 1999.

Smith, Hale G. *Analysis of the Lamar Site (9 Bi 7) Materials at the Southeastern Archaeological Center*. Tallahassee: Florida State University, 1973. See especially "Notes and Sketches on the Development of Ocmulgee National Monument and the Lamar Site," iii–iv.

Stiggins, George. *Creek Indian History: A Historical Narrative of the Genealogy, Traditions and Downfall of the Ispocaga or Creek Indian Tribe of Indians* [sic]. Tuscaloosa: University of Alabama Press for the Birmingham Library Free Press, 1989.

Winn, William W. *The Triumph of the* Ecunnau-Nuxulgee: *Land Speculators, George M. Troup, State Rights, and the Removal of the Creek Indians from Georgia and Alabama*. Macon: Mercer University Press, 2015.

Wright, J. Leitch. *Creeks and Seminoles: The Destruction and Regeneration of the Muscogulge People*. Lincoln: University of Nebraska Press, 1986.

PART 6

KEEPING OCMULGEE

Historical sources quoted in this chapter derive from the *Macon Telegraph*, the press clippings file at Ocmulgee National Monument, and Ocmulgee's Curatorial Department.

Anthes, Bill. "'Why Injun Artist Me': Acee Blue Eagle's Diasporic Performative." In *Native Diasporas: Indigenous Identities and Settler Colonialism in the Americas*, edited by Gregory D. Smithers and Brooke N. Newman, 411-441. Lincoln: University of Nebraska Press, 2014.

Hyatt, Richard. *Charles H. Jones: A Biography*. Macon: Mercer University Press, 2003.

Innes, Pamela. "Creek in the West." In *Handbook of North American Indians: Volume 14, Southeast*, edited by William C. Sturtevant, 393-403. Washington, DC: Smithsonian Institution, 2004.

Mihesuah, Devon. *Repatriation Reader: Who Owns American Indian Remains?* Lincoln: University of Nebraska Press, 2000.

Oppermann, Joseph K. *Ocmulgee Visitor Center: Historic Structure Report*. Washington, DC: National Park Service, 2009.

PART 7
EPILOGUE

Documents related to the museum redesign can be found in Ocmulgee National Monument's Curatorial Department.

Anthes, Bill. *Edgar Heap of Birds*. Durham: Duke University Press, 2015.

SELECT NATIVE LITERATURE OF THE SOUTHEAST

Grantham, Bill. *Creation Myths and Legends of the Creek Indians*. Gainesville: University Press of Florida, 2002.

Haag, Marcia, ed. *A Listening Wind: Native Literature from the Southeast*. Lincoln: University of Nebraska Press, 2016.

Martin, Jack B., et al., eds. Totkv Mocvse / *New Fire: Creek Folktales by Earnest Gouge*. Norman: University of Oklahoma Press, 2005.

Posey, Alexander. *Chinubbie and the Owl: Muscogee (Creek) Stories, Orations, and Oral Traditions*. Lincoln: University of Nebraska Press, 2005.

Swanton, John R. *Myths and Tales of the Southeastern Indians*. Norman: University of Oklahoma Press, 1995. First published 1929.

OCMULGEE NATIONAL MONUMENT

INDEX

A

Adair, James, 99, 101
African Americans
    as New Deal workers, 124, 126
    as slaves, 2, 103, 112, 115
alligators, 19, 65, 85
animals (see also individual animal names), 18, 19, 20, 21, 22, 23, 56, 57, 62, 63, 65, 75, 78, 89, 102
Apalachees, 80, 94–97
Apalachicolas, 81, 84, 94–95
Archaic era, 7, 9, 14, 15, 16, 17–21, 23–24, 25, 26

B

Bartram, William, 2, 4, 81–83, 84, 87
beaver, 158
Beaver, Fred, 86
Beaver, John, 170–71, 174
Bigman, Daniel, 45, 162
Black Drink, 55, 86, 87
Blue Eagle, Acee, 135–37, 140–41, 144–45
Brown's Mount, 48, 124
Bureau of Indian Affairs (BIA), 86, 151, 153, 155

C

Cahokia, 33–34, 38, 45, 48, 52
Central of Georgia (see railroads)
Chattahoochee River, 62, 76, 77, 79, 81, 83–84, 90–91, 95, 97, 99
Checotah, Ben, 151, 153, 155–57
Checotah, Peggy, 151, 156–57
chunkey and chunkey stones, 53, 57, 119
"Civilization" program, 102–03, 105
Civil War (US), 114–16, 120
Civil Works Administration, 123
Civilian Conservation Corps, 124–25, 127, 162
climate, 17, 40, 67, 128
Clovis points, 13, 15, 23, 138
Cornfield Mound, 45, 51
council house (see Earth Lodge)
Cox, Claude, 151, 155, 158
Creeks (see Muskogees)
Creek Week (1972), 157–60

D

Dalton points, 15
dance, 143, 164, 176–77
deer, 10, 18–19, 43, 53, 62, 75, 86, 91–92, 109, 138
Dillahunty, Albert, 148–49
dioramas, 94, 141
Dunlap, Samuel, 111, 114–15, 120

E

eagle, 41, 78–79, 86
Earth Lodge, ix, 8, 38, 40, 41–42, 45, 55, 124–29, 140, 172

F

falcon, 41–42, 57, 85
Fairbanks, Charles, 5, 77, 127, 145
firearms, 80, 91, 92, 95, 145
food, 18, 20, 26, 27, 34, 35, 52, 53, 59, 67–68, 69, 74–75, 85, 89, 142, 144, 147–48, 158
Fort Hawkins, 46, 102–03, 108, 110
Funeral Mound, 5, 23–24, 38–39–40, 45, 48, 57, 61, 100, 116, 123, 138, 146

G

George, Addie, 151–52
Georgia (English colony and American state), 98, 99, 103, 105–06, 108–9, 111, 117, 144, 153, 155, 160, 175
Great Britain (and British Colonization), xv, 9, 68, 80–84, 90–91, 92–98, 102, 114
Great Temple Mound, ix, 12, 23, 35, 37–38, 42, 45–46, 48–49, 51–52, 120, 138, 148, 167, 172, 198
Green Corn ceremonialism, 55, 85, 87, 141, 177
Guy, Millard T., 137–38

H

Harjo, Gerald, 150–53, 155–56, 158
Harris, Walter, 122–24, 130, 148
Harrold, C. C., 123–24
Hawkins, Benjamin, 105, 107
Heap of Birds, Hock E Aye Vi / Edgar, 172–73

I

Ichisi, 59, 63–64, 67–72, 90
Indians (see specific peoples)
Irwin, Carol (see Mason, Carol)

J

Jefferson, Thomas, 102–03, 107
Jenkins, Ned (see dioramas)
Jones, Charles (modern real estate developer), 151, 153, 155
Jones, Charles Colcock Jr., 5, 116–120

K

Kelly, Arthur, 13, 15, 26–27, 39–40, 123, 125, 127
Kolomoki, 48, 146

L

Lamar site (see also Ichisi), xiv, 10, 58–60, 63, 66, 68–69, 71–72, 77, 124–26, 139–40, 175
Lesser Temple Mound, 38–39, 46, 48, 51, 59, 113, 138, 172, 198
Lucas, James, 92–93

M

Macon, xiii–xiv, 2, 10, 70, 72, 77, 110–15, 122, 124, 127–28, 130, 132, 135, 137–38, 140–41, 143, 144–46, 148–51, 153, 155–60, 163, 165, 172, 175–76
Macon Telegraph, 5, 31, 110, 140
Marsh, Alan, 162
Mason, Carol (Irwin), 5, 81, 145
Master Farmers (see Mississippians)
Mateos, Antonio, 80
McGillivray, Alexander, 102
Mercer University, 5, 140–41, 153, 156
Meriwether, Carolyn, 39–40, 61
Micco, Hopoy, 107
Mico, Hoboithle, 104–05, 104
Mico, Hopothle, 104
Middle Georgia State University (formerly Macon State College and Macon Junior College), 153, 162
Mississippians and Mississippian era, 2, 7, 9, 32–41, 44–46, 48–49, 50–61, 97, 114, 138
    art, 53, 55–57
    burial practices, 39–40, 57
    dispersal, 61, 66–68
    economies, 54
    gender roles, 52, 54–55
    houses, v, 51
    diet, 34, 52, 67, 147–48
    governance, 34, 44, 45, 51–52, 54, 57, 59, 67, 70, 71
    military practice, 54
    religious beliefs, 54–57
    mounds (see also specific mound entries), 26, 31, 34, 35, 46, 59, 81, 85, 103, 110–12, 119, 122–23, 130, 133
        construction, 32, 36, 38, 45, 46, 59
        damage, 38–39, 111–14, 116, 119, 120, 131
        location, 35, 48, 49, 111
        meaning, 39, 45–46, 48, 49, 50, 88, 108, 110
Moundbuilder myth, 31–32
Mound A (see Great Temple Mound)
Mound B (see Lesser Temple Mound)
Mound C (see Funeral Mound)
Moundville, 76–77
Museum and Visitor Center, 6, 7, 8, 32, 56, 59, 60, 131, 133, 138–39, 140, 150, 152

    construction, 131–32, 137
    opening, 10, 133, 135, 137, 139–40, 142–43, 146
    redesign, 171–72
Muskogean, xiii, 1, 58, 60, 83, 84
Muskogees (Creeks), 2, 8, 10, 45, 77, 83, 84, 90, 97, 103, 108, 166–67, 93, 171, 174–75
    1950s visits to Ocmulgee, 133, 134, 136–37, 140–46
    Civil War (Creek), 107
    connection to Mississippians, 44–45, 49, 53, 55, 83–4, 85–86, 88, 108
    cosmology, 9, 169
    dance, 143, 176–77
    food, 147
    gender roles, 142–43
    language of, xv, 58, 81, 92
    migration legend of, 4, 49, 81–3
    mounds and, 88, 110, 121, 169, 175–76
    names/naming of, xv–xvi, 72, 84
    origins of, 50, 83, 97
    stickball, 11, 86, 143
    removal, 10, 108–10, 120, 172, 174
    revitalization in 1970s, 149–50
    stories/storytellers, 12, 44, 50, 77–79, 88–90, 169
    tattooing of, 87
    towns/talwas, 9, 81, 83, 90
    treaties, 82, 97, 102, 104, 106–8
    work at Ocmulgee in the 1970s, 150–53, 155–58, 160

N

National Park Service, 6, 8, 10, 81, 123, 137, 140–41, 148–51, 174
Native Americans (see specific peoples)
Native American slavery, 64, 68, 70–71, 91–93
Native American Graves Protection and Repatriation Act (NAGPRA), 146, 166
Nixon, Richard M., 157–58

O

Ocmulgee Indian Celebration, 162, 164–165, 172
Ocmulgee National Monument (see also Museum and Visitor Center, and individual architectural features, e. g. Great Temple Mound)
    "All Things Are Connected" motto, 160

archaeological work at, 13–14, 23–25, 34–39, 45, 51, 59, 77, 81, 92, 116–20, 122–30, 145, 149, 162–63, 166, 172
creation of, 122–23
Drake's Field, 81, 162, 121–22
early museum, 130–31
economic activity at (1800s–1930s), 111, 114–15, 119–121
Eisenhower Parkway Extension, 163
handbook, 6, 7, 8
human remains, 114, 132, 146–47, 166
Interstate 16, 15, 148–49
maps of, viii–ix, 36
Muskogees and (since 1930s), 133, 134, 136–37, 140–46, 150–53, 155–58, 160
orientation of, viii–ix, 48
possible National Park status, 174–75
as sacred ground, 2, 48, 84, 99, 107, 111, 121, 129, 136–37, 163, 167
sale of lands (1828), 110–11
Traditional Cultural Property (TCP) status, 163–64
Ocmulgee River, xiii–xiv, 1–4, 17, 19–20, 28, 31, 53, 63, 69, 71, 73–75, 81–84, 90–93, 97, 99–100, 103, 105–7, 109–10, 112–13, 115, 120–21, 147–49, 176
Ocmulgee to Okmulgee Ride, 170, 174
Okmulgee, Oklahoma, 140, 171–72
Ocute, 60, 63, 66–68, 71–72
Oglethorpe, James, 4
owl, 19, 21–23

R

Paleoindians and Paleoindian era, 7, 9, 13–17, 21, 23, 25
panther, 19, 57, 85
Pope, G. D. ("Gus") Jr., 6–8, 16, 18, 32–33, 77
pottery, 21, 23–27, 34, 52, 57, 58, 60, 76–77, 92, 138, 140, 145, 156, 158, 172

Q

Queen Anne's War, 94–97

R

railroads, 2, 12, 36, 38–39, 42–43, 111–20, 121, 149
Revolutionary War (see War for Independence)
Roosevelt, Franklin Delano, 123, 139

S

Smith, Sibbald, 162
Solomon, Linton, 123–24
de Soto, Hernando, 4, 10, 60–71
Southeast Archaeological Center (SEAC), 149
Spain and Spanish colonization (see also Hernando de Soto), 4, 59, 63, 66, 69, 76, 79–81, 84, 90–98, 102
stickball, 86, 141, 143–44, 165, 172
Swanson, James T., 140
Swift Creek, 26–28, 48

T

Tiger, George, 169–70, 174
torture, 95–96
Trading Post (1690s–1710s), 5, 43, 81, 91–94, 97–98, 114, 116, 124, 139, 145–46, 162
Trading Post (1970s), 150–52

V

Vinson, Carl, 123, 148–49
Visitor Center (see Museum and Visitor Center)

W

war and warfare (see also specific names of conflicts), 54, 57, 82–83, 86, 93–94, 96–97, 101, 115–16, 131, 140, 166
War for Independence (American), 10, 102
Waring, Antonio C., Jr., 13
Woodland peoples and era, 9, 14, 21, 25–28, 48, 57, 138
Woodward, Henry, 80
Works Progress Administration, 123, 128

Y

Yamasees, 72, 97
Yamasee War, 82–83, 93, 96–98
yaupon holly, 86–87
Yuchis, 49–50, 90, 151–52

TEMPLE MOUNDS Present-day view, looking southeast, of the Great Temple Mound (right) and the Lesser Temple Mound at Ocmulgee National Monument. (Courtesy Sharman Ayoub.)

OCMULGEE NATIONAL MONUMENT